Managing Microcomputers in Large Organizations

Board on Telecommunications
and Computer Applications

Commission on Engineering
and Technical Systems

National Research Council

NATIONAL ACADEMY PRESS
Washington, D.C.   1985

NATIONAL ACADEMY PRESS   2101 CONSTITUTION AVE., NW   WASHINGTON, DC 20418

NOTICE: The project that is the subject of this report was approved by the Governing Board of the National Research Council, whose members are drawn from the councils of the National Academy of Sciences, the National Academy of Engineering, and the Institute of Medicine. The members of the committee responsible for the forum were chosen for their special competences and with regard for appropriate balance.

This report has been reviewed by a group other than the authors according to procedures approved by a Report Review Committee consisting of members of the National Academy of Sciences, the National Academy of Engineering, and the Institute of Medicine.

The National Research Council was established by the National Academy of Sciences in 1916 to associate the broad community of science and technology with the Academy's purposes of furthering knowledge and of advising the federal government. The Council operates in accordance with general policies determined by the Academy under the authority of its congressional charter of 1863, which establishes the Academy as a private, nonprofit, self-governing membership corporation. The Council has become the principal operating agency of both the National Academy of Sciences and the National Academy of Engineering in the conduct of their services to the government, the public, and the scientific and engineering communities. It is administered jointly by both Academies and the Institute of Medicine. The National Academy of Engineering and the Institute of Medicine were established in 1964 and 1970, respectively, under the charter of the National Academy of Sciences.

Library of Congress Cataloging in Publication Data

Board on Telecommunications and Computer Applications,
   Commission on Engineering and Technical Systems,
   National Research Council.
   Managing microcomputers in large organizations.
   Includes index.
   1. Business—Data processing—Management—Congresses.
2. Office practice—Automation—Management—Congresses.
3. Microcomputers—Congresses. I. National Research
Council (U.S.) Board on Telecommunications and
Computer Applications.
HF5548.2.M297   1985   658'.054   84-22617
ISBN 0-309-03492-2

Printed in the United States of America

Preface and Acknowledgments

Most people in the business of information management had been expecting microcomputers for years. Yet their arrival in the Christmas season of 1981 took many by surprise. It was another example of technology being in advance of our ability to use it and to manage it. Since that time, further technological advances have made microcomputers more powerful, more economical, and simpler to use. These so-called personal computers have spawned a revolution in the way information is gathered and exchanged.

For large organizations the revolution means a basic change in the relationship of end users to central computing facilities. Until recently end users depended on data processing specialists to create and operate their programs. With new development in personal computers and software, however, end users are growing more and more independent of the specialists: Many professionals with no prior experience in data processing have introduced personal computers into their working lives.

The proliferation of microcomputers has overwhelmed many organizations and in the process created two serious problems for management: How do we control the headlong transition from centralized to decentralized computation without stifling the creativity of the end user? And how do we manage the use of microcomputers to enhance productivity and make the organization's total computing capability cost-effective?

The National Research Council's Board on Telecommunications and Computer Applications held a forum in late 1983 to address these and related concerns. The meeting featured experts from two broad areas of experience: senior executives from the private and public sectors who have directed the use of computers in their own companies or in the federal government, and technology innovators who are directly responsible for the increasing popularity of personal computers.

This book is the product of that meeting. Written by and for executives, it probes these questions: Where is microcomputer technology going? What are the implications of these directions for large organizations? What are the emerging issues critical to top management? And how are selected large organizations dealing with these issues?

Many people shared in the creation of this book. In particular, I wish to thank the members of our steering committee (see page viii) and the contributing authors. Staff members of the Board on Telecommunications and Computer Applications who organized the forum—Jerome D. Rosenberg, senior staff officer and forum director; and Lois A. Leak, administrative secretary—also deserve special thanks, as does Paula Kaufmann, who edited the transcript of the meeting.

I also wish to recognize and thank our sponsors: Arthur Young and Company, the Tennessee Valley Authority, the U.S. Department of Defense, the U.S. General Services Administration, and the U.S. Veterans Administration.

Francis A. McDonough*
Chairman

---

*Francis A. McDonough is deputy assistant administrator of the Office of Information Resources Management, U.S. General Services Administration. He championed the development of the federal government's Managed Innovation Program, which is fully described in Chapter 9.

Contents

v

Steering Committee
Managing Microcomputers in Large Organizations

OVERVIEW

Vision and Value

Getting the Most out of Microcomputers

*John M. Thompson**

I believe we are now in the second wave of the computer revolution. The first wave focused on the use of information technology to *replace* people; now we are more concerned with *supporting* people. We are moving from the automation of structured tasks of the first 10 to 15 years of the computer revolution into the support of unstructured tasks, the support of managerial activity.

Much of the discussion in this book concerning end-user computing and managerial support uses words and ideas that have been around for years. Now, however, different media and technologies are available. In the late 1960s we saw timesharing; in the 1970s, minicomputers; in the early 1980s, the information centers—a sort of in-house timesharing service bureau. Now in the mid-1980s, we are seeing an influx of personal computers (PCs), end-user computing, and networks. There is a lot of talk about the need to integrate all of these technologies to support people in their workplace.

John Diebold sets the stage for this discussion when he talks about the millions of computer-literate people in the workplace for whom microcomputers can unleash imaginations and creativity. He also reminds us of the proliferation of technological alterna-

---

*John M. Thompson is vice-president of Index Systems, Inc., Cambridge, Massachusetts.

tives with a rather catchy phrase: "option shock." The theme of unleashing creativity recurs throughout this book. In the industrial revolution we invented machines to provide leverage to human muscle; perhaps now we are inventing machines that can provide leverage to the human mind. To carry the analogy a little further, in the nineteenth century we provided support to the blue-collar worker; in the twentieth century we have been providing support to the white-collar worker. Some time early in the twenty-first century we must find a way to bring it all together.

The essays in Part I examine where microcomputer technology has come from and where it appears to be headed. Thomas Willmott discusses what he calls the "technology push" in his description of the first two phases in the evolution of the personal computer. In the first phase the personal computer is simply an individual workstation. It is characterized by a cottage industry of software producers supplying the workstation and trying to make it useful. Now we are moving into a second phase, in which microcomputers become part of a network. This phase raises many kinds of different problems that are echoed in this report: Where is the data? How do I manage it? How do I exercise control? Do I control? Willmott, as well as other contributors to this volume, evokes the image of some bright scientists making machines faster, cheaper, and smaller and then pushing them into our organizations, saying, "There! You figure out what to do with them!"

The notion of "technology push" is reinforced by Mitchell Kapor, who writes about the "heroic geniuses" producing software. Software producers are not driven by a careful analysis of market need, says Kapor. Instead, they are driven by the need simply to figure out what to do with the personal computer. Because nobody really knows what to do with these computers, somebody gets a good idea, tries it, and perhaps it works in the marketplace.

Kapor predicts that soon the general drive will be toward software systems that integrate five major areas of microcomputer use—spreadsheet, data base, word processing, graphics, and communications. New developments will allow easy movement between windows and create open systems that can interact with other hardware and applications software systems—in which each of the five elements is not compromised by being part of an integrated system. The design objectives of such systems is to produce individual applications that are just as good as the available stand-alone versions. In addition, the "home" of the data would be absolutely transparent to the user. For those of us who have used any form of a personal computing system, be it a personal computer or distributed from a timesharing system, this all sounds very powerful. In fact, combining the power of the technology in both hardware and software seems a little like having a Ferrari on the island of Grenada. Right now PCs make a great deal of power available, but there are not many places for us to use that power yet.

Robert Metcalfe predicts widespread use of local area networks with peripheral sharing, information access, and personal communications. Some have predicted that the 1980s will be remembered as the critical decade in which everyone became interconnected. If this is the case, it is apparent that the communications applications of microcomputers will become increasingly important. We can expect communications to emerge as one of the critical issues of the mid-1980s.

Part II of this report probes the implications of this technology push. John Bennett discusses its meaning for the managers of information systems (IS). In short, the IS manager must improve service or lose. Bennett describes some of the tools now available to the manager to improve the productivity of the IS department. He also describes the reactions of IS managers to the rapid growth in microcomputer use occurring in their companies: Proliferation inevitably raises the issue of control, specifically control of data. To those who ask the question "Why control?" the answer heard most often is: "Because in two years' time the data that is recognized as a critical resource of this corporation will not be in my machine, but will be on everybody else's desk. My chief executive is going to turn to me and say, 'How in the world did you ever get us into this mess?' "

Bennett also points out that a major part of the job of the IS manager is to open the gates and facilitate access to corporate data by a variety of different systems, including microcomputers. Related to this is the need for IS managers to take responsibility for educating management. Although it is a significant departure from their traditional role of information processing, more and more the responsibility of IS managers to educate is being termed critical to their success. Bennett outlines a very successful program at United Technologies to educate 1,000 senior managers.

Finally, Bennett raises the issue of security as one of the major worries of the IS manager. Horror stories abound in this area. I know one IS manager who put his career in jeopardy by walking around his executive suite and picking up floppy disks left on the top of file cabinets. When he took them back to his office, he found that he had all of the corporation's recent and projected financial data, the latest competitive analysis, and some sensitive data about personnel salaries for the leading 100 people in the corporation. People were leaving sensitive data around on floppy disks that they would never leave around on a piece of paper. This represents a whole different set of security issues from what we have dealt with for the last 20 years in managing information systems, and we have to learn the differences fast. By 1990 the workstation will probably be as common as the telephone. Managing this change has significant implications for organizations.

Ray Kline reports on what the federal government is doing in its Managed Innovation Program. His "stick-and-carrot" metaphor is particularly appropriate to describe the control-support system of the government's program. While the imposition of standards and restrictions on users is necessary, users can be offered in return more support for their work. Such support includes easier procurement procedures, and new tools for education.

James Bair examines some of the implications of small computer technology for managerial support. He describes a major shift away from a very specialized awareness in information technology to a mass awareness in our society and the implications of this shift within corporations and between corporations and society.

Bair also underlines the importance of communications and the need for the microcomputer business to support communications. This idea has been echoed by many others in the field of executive support. In the early days we coined the term "decision support system." In the late 1960s and early 1970s we had a rather naive notion that decisions were the executive activity that needed support. Later research pointed out, however, that executives spend far more time communicating than making decisions. Instead of decision support systems we must talk about communications support systems, or perhaps learning support systems, or management support systems, or just plain support systems. The real task is to bridge the gap between technology and people by understanding what people do that needs supporting.

Jim Bair gives us another insight in this area. He says he has spent a great deal of time trying to figure out how to measure productivity, only to discover that nobody wants to measure it anymore. I suspect that many of us have as an objective the improvement of "productivity," something we have not defined and cannot measure. We all intuitively understand that using the technology to improve productivity is a worthy objective. But what does that mean? How do you know when you've done it? How does it apply to our organizations? There is an increased reluctance to hone in on what productivity is. At the same time there is a great move to double it!

Part III explores some specific and vital management issues. Alastair Omand—one of the few senior IS people who report to the executive committee of a very large corporation—believes there are two major issues raised by microcomputers in organizations that the chief executive officer (CEO) should really worry about. The first is data management and its associated problems of accessibility, compatibility, and security. For this he recommends putting a person in a position of organizational responsibility for the corporation's data. The CEO's second worry is the shift in skill sets—another variation on the persistent theme of education. Other contributors deal with this theme from the perspective of the effects of microcomputers on the entire culture of the organization, but the point made by all of the contributors is that top management, and chief executives in particular, must worry about how this technology will change their organizations. Their users must become developers and managers. They must keep up with shifting technical trends and watch for the changing role of information systems in their organizations.

Other important issues, according to Omand, should be left to the line management of the organization to handle. Product proliferation, or "option shock," as John Diebold calls it, causes concern about "connectivity." Will we be able to interconnect everyone? Will we be able to supply adequate technical support? Will we have huge duplication of effort between people who do not talk to each other in the organization? Omand recommends that we leave these problems to the users, keeping them in charge, letting them take advantage of technological change.

Acquisition practice raises another set of concerns. There are questions about cost justification and how to achieve good cost savings, what interface to have with vendors, buying equipment that becomes obsolete very fast, and trouble with license restric-

tions on software. For all of these very real issues Omand recommends that the chief executive officer make use of existing
mechanisms like the purchasing department and the control
mechanisms through the budget.

Roger Sisson views the discussion on microcomputers as really
a discussion about end-user computing. He suggests that putting
motivated people together with good tools and relevant data will
produce what he calls "distributed creativity." In other words,
looking at data seems to facilitate innovative thinking.

Distributed creativity is not a term that would have fared very
well in the early 1970s. A decade later, however, we are getting
used to this sort of concept. It is tied in with the theme of unleashing creativity and the notion that something very fundamental is
now going on that we do not really understand. It has been
brought on by new tools, data, and the technology push.

Part IV presents a number of case studies that suggest the possibilities for dealing—on a day-to-day basis—with the challenges
of the microcomputer revolution. Norman Epstein sees control as
the overriding concern for management. From this comes his concept of personal comput*ing* rather than personal comput*ers*.
Other contributors to this section suggest alternative approaches
to the dual questions of control and support. In most cases the
vehicle chosen is less important than what actually happens in
support of people.

Several essays in this volume refer to Gibson and Nolan's
stages of growth curve, which can also be called a technology
learning curve. Gibson and Nolan first published their article on
the four stages of growth at a time when we were approaching
maturity in the earliest—data processing—technology learning
curve. We are now on another technology learning curve involv-
ing personal computing.

We hear much talk about the first and third stages on this
curve: getting started, and getting control. We do not find many
people worrying about the second stage, getting value. Perhaps
this is because value is a difficult word that, like productivity,
defies definition and measurement. But the question will not go
away. Why are the technology pushers doing this to us, and what
value can we get out of it for whom?

I believe value can be derived for at least three levels of people
in organizations, but for each level opportunities are different. As
the leader of the organization, the senior executive can set the

culture and change the organization. At another level, the functional managers need to develop an intuition about the business—about what works and what doesn't work. By and large, they are the people who achieve the operating results of the organization. At a third level, there are analysts who are clearly the prime target for the new tools of the technology. How are we to derive value for these three defined users of microcomputer technology? Do we rely on some sort of invisible hand? Should we merely give them the tools and say, "Go do something useful with this elegant technology?" To what extent should we focus on data management, on security, on controls, on education concerning what the tool can do?

We are left with many unanswered questions. However, I would be amazed if they were answered at this stage because I do not think that we yet know where we are going with the technology. And if you don't know where you are going you can get there any way you like.

These papers reflect the candor of informed experts in the field who are not afraid to admit that "we don't know where we are going." There's an old Zen saying: "In the mind of the beginner, there are infinite possibilities; in the mind of the expert, there are very few." Right now, we should beware of experts who claim to have all the answers; at this stage we really can't know what we are getting into.

Perhaps one word we need to hear more often is "vision." Organizations must have a strategic purpose for this technology. They must head toward some goal. As a whole, the papers in this volume may present what appears to be a dichotomy between two broad themes. On the one hand, there is the very clear theme of using automation to increase productivity. This goal raises very familiar management issues of planning, organization, and control. The response is relatively straightforward. We can apply the tools of planning and management that we have learned over the last several decades, and they ought to stand us in good stead. We will manage our way through it, if that is where we are going.

On the other hand, some of these authors suggest that our goal has to do with unleashing capability, with leveraging a person's mind, with innovation and creativity. If this is the goal I am not at all sure we know how to manage. Perhaps it is appropriate at this point to hand out tools and say, "You figure out what to do with them." Perhaps this is a time of intelligent experimentation, a "seed time," a period of learning. Or perhaps both approaches should be followed together to see what happens if we unleash the creativity of a million computer-literate people.

Most importantly, I believe we must pause for a moment to examine what we are trying to accomplish with this technology in our individual organizations, that is, where we want to go. Clearly, something very important and very fundamental is going on that we do not yet fully understand. It is an extraordinarily interesting, stimulating, and exciting time. I am only uncomfortable when I hear people *predicting* their future instead of *choosing* it. This is my argument with the concept of technology push. We must be sure to confront the dichotomy between productivity and creativity. Do we want one or the other? Or do we want both? And what does that mean? We must choose what we want, not just predict what we might get. Depending on our choice, there are fundamentally different implications for different management styles, the changing role of the IS manager, data, security, value, and how to manage in an era of intelligent experimentation.

The attributes of success that many of the contributors to this volume discuss have some common themes. There is the concept of marketing to users. There is the concept of users and the need to provide education and other support systems for them. There are the operational issues of security and data management. There are the finance issues and questions of cost justification. There are some issues of administrative responsibility. Further, there are human resource issues: how do we educate people and what kind of people do we need for this new era?

These are, in fact, the major headings for a business plan: marketing, operations, finance, administration, human resources. But this is a plan for a business within the business. It is the business of making microcomputers or any personal computing technology work to support the people within the organization. Like any business, its primary objective is getting business value. This must be the ultimate objective for us all.

The Organizational Issues

John Diebold *

From a management perspective, three important points can be made about the phenomenon of microcomputer proliferation we are now witnessing. The first is that we stand at a milestone. The ever-increasing computer literacy of our society has altered the way one thinks about microprocessors, as well as the role of information technology in any large organization. Daily there are front page items in the newspapers indicating that the role of the computer in society has changed from what it was only two or three years ago. The 414s—the infamous Milwaukee-area "hackers" who take their name from their telephone area code—are a marvelous symptom of this change.

The difference is due not simply to larger numbers of micros. The situation is different because we have reached a critical mass in society. There are now millions of computer-literate people who are doing new kinds of things with this tool. This is a very different environment in which to place the role of information processing.

The second point, and a crucial issue, is whether an organization should adopt a control mentality toward microprocessors or whether it should take a very different approach. The alternative

*John Diebold is chairman and founder of the Diebold Group, Inc., New York, New York.

11

approach encourages a much more permissive environment so that individuals may develop many more uses and roles for micros within the organization.

Until recently, information processing meant an essentially institutionalized structure in which the individual had little choice in what he or she did in minute-to-minute applications—what the psychologists of the workplace call nondiscretionary work. This is changing. Information processing is making labor very discretionary. Such a shift raises a number of questions. What is an organization's management policy on microprocessors? Do they become a symbol of this transformation, the unleashing of imaginations, the extending of an employee's capabilities? Or are they in essence controlled? These two approaches represent fundamentally different management styles and philosophies, and organizations must analyze them thoroughly before adopting one or the other.

We should not assume that the same approaches and management philosophy applied to information technology up to this point can or must apply in the future. Most of the literature, as well as most management approaches, treats information processing as a support function. In many cases it is still a support function, but in more and more organizations it is becoming a line activity. It is essential to recognize this change. No longer is it a question of thinking about an orderly or a cost-justified approach to information processing. That is not how personal computers (PCs) are justified or bought. They are bought through every conceivable means for all kinds of applications. Only a minimum number of these purchases are justified according to the sort of highly developed methodology that exists for conventional data processing.

Microcomputers are also being purchased in gigantic quantities, with far-reaching implications. The stand-alone personal computer is a transitory phenomenon, but it happens to dominate at the moment. The most recent surveys indicate that only about one-fifth of micros now in use are connected to larger systems. This obviously will change, and it will become the norm to put these micros into many kinds of informal as well as formal networks.

We must also recognize that the microprocessor joins the game while there are five loose pieces on the organizational playing board. These pieces and their relationship to management decisions about microcomputers are the third key point I would emphasize.

One of these loose pieces is the traditionally managed *data processing activity*. This activity normally reports at a middle-to-high-level management structure and has a quite highly developed methodology and control mechanism.

The second loose piece is the *communications* function, which normally has reported at a lower level because there haven't been very many options. Now, however, the communications area is experiencing what some are calling "option shock" in response to the vast number of communications options available. As a result, an enormous burden of network design, previously borne by the principal outside supplier, AT&T, has been placed on the large user. The entire communications function is changing very rapidly.

The third piece on the board is the *office automation* function. This area has typically reported at a lower level than the data processing activity and has been oriented towards clerical savings. In reality, however, office automation should support professional activities. This is beginning to occur.

A fourth piece is the area of *manufacturing systems*, where major changes in the whole approach to manufacturing are occurring as a result of information technology. Although several organizational models exist in this area, Diebold Research Program studies have shown that it has normally reported separately. Now, however, manufacturing systems are starting to be consolidated with other information processing functions.

The fifth piece is the largest and most important—the *end user*. The end-user level is the point at which many microcomputers are now being acquired. For example, one of our clients recently bought 10,000 PCs, with an escalator clause to go to 30,000. In fact, most large organizations are purchasing micros by the thousands, but they are doing so in smaller increments.

Until now only 3 percent of the data processing education budget has been spent on end users. As a result, employees are currently spending a lot of time educating themselves. Obviously this situation must change dramatically. End-user education is where the bulk of the future data processing (DP) training budget will have to be spent. All of the traditional statistics on DP spending ignore this end-user area. Thus, the actual level of investment of an organization for data processing is quite different than the traditional budget figures might show, because it is with the end user that developments are occurring.

These five organizational pieces have been floating, and organizations have tried to deal with them in different ways. Although the right approach depends on the organization and its mission the role of information technology in that mission is itself changing because the parameters of competition are changing. Industry lines are shifting. These shifts are most apparent in the financial service fields, in publishing and broadcasting, and now in retailing as computers move into the home.

Changes are also beginning to occur in the parameters of competition within individual industries. This means that management must think less about management information systems and more about business information systems. As information flows from the raw data stage through all the stages to the end user, previously discrete activities become intertwined.

What I mean to suggest is that today, all is in flux, and it is against this changing and developing background that management must think about the role of microcomputers.

PART I
SMALL COMPUTER TECHNOLOGY
Where We Are and Where We're Headed

Introduction

William H. Leary III*

There are few, if any, precedents for the microcomputer explosion. It has surprised most of us and is now recognized as a major force of change in small and large organizations alike. Microcomputers are spreading rapidly into every walk of life. Unfortunately, such growth makes it difficult to identify clear trends and other underlying forces. The authors of the next three chapters are uniquely qualified to assess the status of and trends in microcomputer technology.

Thomas Willmott of International Data Corporation begins with a broad review that gathers the threads of hardware, software, and communications into a fabric that explains the direction of the microcomputer/personal computer industry. He represents that special group of industry observers who can help us understand what is happening.

The other authors, Mitchell Kapor and Robert Metcalfe, are leaders among the small number of visionary geniuses in the microcomputer industry. Kapor, whose software products include the enormously successful 1-2-3 as well as Visitrend and Visiplot, shares his observations on where microcomputer software is heading and looks at the apparent conflict between the successful

*William H. Leary III is deputy director, Information Resources Management Systems, Office of the Assistant Secretary of Defense.

17

software entrepreneur and the organizational needs of the software companies as they grow larger.

Robert Metcalfe of 3Com Corporation is the well-known inventor of the Ethernet local area network technology and a major figure in microcomputer communications. He reviews the status and future of the increasingly important networking potential of microcomputers.

Together, these three chapters offer an important perspective on the problems and potential of microcomputer technology.

Faster, Smaller, Cheaper
Trends in Microcomputer Technology
Thomas H. Willmott*

At International Data Corporation we do market research and competitive analysis for both vendors and users of information processing equipment. Therefore, when I look at where the technology has been and where it is going, I see it from two viewpoints: where the industry is moving and how well users are adapting to the changes. But from both viewpoints the movement can be summarized in three words: faster, smaller, and cheaper.

As we look at the past and future of microcomputers it may be helpful to think in terms of a microcomputer's life cycle. I would suggest that there are three phases to this cycle. The first is hardware introduction, during which time users have the opportunity to review hardware capabilities. The second phase is the response to that original debut—whether it attracts peripheral vendors of hardware and stimulates software development that provides a wide and rich work environment. No corporation, not even IBM, can stand alone in this marketplace. All need the diversity of the expansion board vendors, the software vendors, the whole new industry that has emerged over the last few years. Thus, in the second phase it is critical to sense whether the new machine is

---

*Thomas H. Willmott is director of user programs and a personal computer analyst for International Data Corporation, Framingham, Massachusetts.

attracting the needed kind of support. If it is, the third phase may extend well beyond the technologically useful life of the machine. It may not be the smartest processor on the block, but because of its installed base of software and its range of capabilities it is sufficient to the task at hand for the two, three, or four years needed to amortize the equipment.

If we think in historical terms, it's obvious that what we have seen so far in personal computers and microcomputers is merely an introduction to what will be coming. In the early 1960s mainframe computers were placed behind plate-glass windows and handled by men and women in white coats. Approaching the data processing facility was like going to the mountain, which Mohammed had to do, even if he was the president of the corporation. In its first stage of development the personal computer, too, was seen as a curiosity. End users found themselves relatively unprepared in technological terms to deal with microcomputers in any meaningful way. The industry had to translate the buzzwords for the end-user group; the technology, though smaller, was still rather exotic.

In this first stage we dealt with the personal computer as an individual workstation, as an independent processing unit rather than as part of a larger organizational framework. Looked upon perhaps as a toy by the MIS (management information systems) department, it was viewed with suspicion, as something that wasn't really part of the computer resources facility. We also had to deal with the whole area of shared peripherals, secondary to whatever unit was on the desk. A Winchester disk that cost $2,500, for example, was difficult to justify for a microcomputer that sold for $1,995. Thus we ended up with rolling resources—printers on a cart, which could be moved around a department and shared among a number of people. This was a rudimentary approach to what would in time become a sophisticated data-processing environment.

During the first stage we also had to explain system software to our end users, as well as come to grips with it in terms of management decisions. One problem was that a single-user operating system was completely foreign to the data processing environments in which our top managers worked. They were used to much more sophisticated operating systems. Since end users had absolutely no experience with system software, we had to teach them how to use it and explain its role in terms of system responsibility. We had to deal with many poor hardware and software decisions made by uneducated end users who purchased equipment for their departments. We found ourselves buying hardware that could not do the job it was assigned to do because application software was dreadfully lacking.

Jean Piaget, a psychologist who specialized in cognitive development, had a theory about individuals being thrown off equilibrium and then assimilating information on a new subject until they reached equilibrium again. In its first stage of development the microcomputer created a similar disequilibrium environment, and only now are end users and managers coming to grips with the issues raised by the microcomputer as a small, cheap workstation.

During this first stage we also had to deal with how application software was going to be defined and developed. Would it focus on task-specific, horizontal packages such as database managers, word processors, and spreadsheets? Or would the thrust be for vertical markets, where an application could be developed that solved a total business problem? In terms of horizontal packages, we began to move from single-function to integrated software. In the vertical market there was less progress because there were fewer opportunities both from a research and development standpoint and from a financial, business standpoint.

Hardware was still a precious resource in this first stage. Memory was a governing factor. The 8-bit CP/M operating system and a number of software graphics packages based on 8-bit technology were designed to do somersaults within a small space because memory and disk storage capacities were at a premium. Stage-one hardware was supported by a cottage industry of software programmers who appeared highly suspect to large companies and federal agencies. One of these new companies, with perhaps 10 to 12 employees, would have the hottest package in the world but a balance sheet that would make your personal checkbook look proud. We were not used to doing business with these kinds of firms.

As we moved toward the end of stage one we began to take a look at what else we could do with a microcomputer. We had figured out what it could do for us locally; now we began to look at the larger environment: the corporation as a whole, the federal agency, the state government computing resource.

In the second stage of microcomputer development, which is

where we are today, we are more likely to see the microcomputer as a window on a greater distributed resource system. Today we look out from our microcomputers and talk either to a mainframe, a strip-file on a minicomputer, or to a larger communications database technology. We may be tying into other organizations or services, into other resources in our own corporations, or perhaps into a local group of microcomputers, where we can share files in a more sophisticated fashion than ever before. Today the microcomputer is associated more with communications and with computing on a grand scale than it is with the idea of a stand-alone workstation. Processing capabilities are still important at the local level, but concurrent processes are more important. These include multiple windows on the same terminal which allow the user to be active in a job that runs on a mainframe and also to merge that data into local files and manipulate it at local memory levels.

The key issue we are now facing is micro-to-mainframe communication. We are trying to answer questions about how the microcomputer fits into a total computing capability. Where are the remote data? Are they available to the end user? Shall they be made available? How often will they be updated? How does all this affect decision making? The microcomputer is coming of age. In this second stage of development the communications capability will increase rather than decrease; the demands for even broad-band communications links may well be in place within the next two years.

The whole area of microprocessor technology, peripheral chips, and small circuit technology in general has brought additional pressures to bear on the MIS or ADP (automated data processing) planning branch. Microcomputers are only one symptom of the total technological wave that is rolling over us. We are being forced to make management changes as well, not only in the area of microcomputer planning and acquisition training, but in our whole ADP planning and telecommunications staff. We have a communications group on one hand, and an ADP planning function on the other. Microprocessor technology and microcomputers have forced an organizational change in the relation between the two types of jobs in the communications area.

Microprocessor technology has in one way made capacity planning obsolete, not in terms of the skills or people required, but simply because movement is no longer from one huge machine to another. Smaller steps are now involved. We are more concerned with how to develop application software across an entire computing resource. Clearly, we have more options in the area of capacity planning than we had several years ago when the only computing facility for a new application was a large mainframe or perhaps a distributed mini with a dedicated voice-grade line. Today we have an entire range of processing capabilities throughout our organizations, ranging from small desktop equipment to much larger machines. The variety of options offered by the new technology means that traditional job functions have to change to maintain efficiency within the organization.

Integrated circuit technology is the driving force of equipment development occurring in the second stage. And we almost have a second generation of the distributed resource, which will include small, local loops of technology (a loop of intelligent workstations or a loop of Apple computers, for example); front ends to large mainframes; twin minis, which handle strip files for management decision making; and remote communications to other networks. Based on effective management decisions concerning cost/benefit analysis, these are the directions in which we will be moving in the mid-1980s in terms of a totally distributed information resource. It is absolutely critical that organizations be concerned not only with the technology but also with how the technology will serve our business, raise our profit levels, and help our service.

I suggest that the key issue to keep in mind when making decisions about the management of computers is that what we are doing with each new level of technology is serving a wider audience of potential users. When we had five people in white coats overseeing the major computer in the computer center, the management problem was relatively easy. We delivered data to the center, pumped it through, and if everything went according to plan, the machine gave us a printout that we could distribute on a rolling cart. Today there is still the need for that kind of application; batch applications for payroll and receivables and data-crunching operations have not gone away. However, as the technology becomes cheaper, we can serve more people with different types of equipment and software.

If we take a look at what has been happening from the vendors' standpoint we find that in the early 1980s the 6502 and the Z80 chips were the key foundations for microcomputer development. Software developers were moving the fastest in these areas and, therefore, they attracted hardware peripheral vendors, additional software development, and user involvement in the applications development process at the site. These two early microprocessors have now been relegated to the sidelines. Their address-based limitations have caused people in the business graphics market, for example, to shift to larger 16- and 32-bit types of hardware. Thus, to purchase the older equipment today may be a bad business decision, though there may be nothing wrong with continuing to use it effectively if we already have it. Because of market dynamics, the purchase of both hardware and software is an important business decision. We don't necessarily want our programmers to have to solve all our application needs. Of course, if we have embedded systems or unique applications, we will want to be able to quickly develop new applications that meet our specifications. But we also want to be able to make use of new applications in the field.

It now appears that the Intel 16-/32-bit chips (the 8088 and perhaps later the 188) may provide some stability in the area of the general-purpose business tool like the IBM PC. However, the Apple McIntosh is coming in at a relatively inexpensive level using the 68000 from Motorola, and others will be fast on its heels as a third generation of application software is developed.

We can anticipate some exciting things for the future. These include object-oriented architectures—dealing in objects rather than continuous lines of code—that move from one object to another and have the kind of transfer talked about in the same breath with artificial intelligence. We will also have additional capabilities on the chip itself, which will give another level of sophistication.

However eagerly we may anticipate such future developments, it is not necessarily best to wait for them to happen. There are many things an organization can do now to improve its productivity, even beyond an individual workstation application to make that device earn its keep. To be concerned about technological obsolescence is a good idea from the standpoint of long-range planning, but it shouldn't prevent us from getting new work done now.

In the near term one of the major technological impacts will be in the area of peripheral chips. This is a key area in terms of the smaller, cheaper, faster syndrome. The ability to put all kinds of sophisticated programming locally at the chip level and integrate it into the workstation gives the user a smaller, cleaner, and more powerful device. This is a characteristic of the second stage. For users stage two means looking out across a larger network of capabilities; for the vendor it means delivering more power at lower cost, with peripheral technology as well as dedicated distributed resources. Modem chips are one example of peripheral chip development; they give the capability to put a modem on an expansion board and simply have a wire attachment coming out of the personal computer. I think peripheral chip technology will make the whole area of word processing protocol conversion a nonissue in two or three years, when we will be able to encode all of a system's character formats and control codes at the chip level—all transparent to the end user.

What is apparent in this discussion of stage-two developments is that vendors have not and managers of computer user environments should not underestimate the demand both for sophisticated devices with interfaces that are easy to use and for powerful microprocessor systems. This demand changes the character of the capacity planning capability that I defined earlier. Where will we deliver the application of software? How will we develop it? Where should it be located in our network of processing capabilities? The question is not how much we can get, but what good use can we put it to? And further, how much raw processing power do we need at the desk? This last question is part of the larger question—where do we need power in our organization?

It is likely that in just a few years, we will walk into a large mainframe computer facility and see 40 people wandering around a processor the size of a file cabinet. A brief look at what is presently available in terms of off-loading power from the mainframe and the minicomputer suggests some of the possibilities for the future:

Lisa. Though I hate rodents and think the Mouse is overrated and takes away from keyboarding capabilities, Lisa suggests the potential of multiple windows. The ability to process numerous applications at one time and to move from one process to another as we would with pieces of paper on our desk is clearly in our future.

Apollo. Apollo represents the workstation of the future. (One is already available for $9,000.) With tremendous horsepower, and capable of relatively simplified artificial intelligence research, Apollo was chosen as the lead system at the Yale Artificial

Intelligence Labs on the basis of cost performance, multiple concurrent processes, and a domain operating system in which a
number of units in the network share their own resources. Rather
than having a mainframe, one key computer facility, Apollo will
have its intelligence distributed around the network, with additional capacity available at any time if needed. Apollo represents
a new philosophy. It defines domain as being able to reach out, not
only to share files but to gain processing power from other workstations.

Synapse.   Another company that has been involved in sharing
processing power is Synapse. With each additional user a microprocessor is added into a back-playing system. The controlling
logic of the system distributes the resources of the microprocessors in the network so that the user is not limited to the power at
the individual workstation.

From a historical perspective, development has clearly been
from mainframe to microcomputer to the concept of the workstation as a window onto a distributed resources network. There
has been development in other directions as well:

Wang.   A recent offering from Wang gives a sense of the other
capabilities that will become available. The new Wang PIC, a
jazzed-up version of its personal computer, works with a charge-
coupled device technology to digitize a piece of paper. The user
places the piece of paper containing graphics on the workstation
platform and presses a button on the keyboard; the bit-map of the
image is blown into a bit-map on the screen and is integrated into
the text capability. Thus we have the integration of text and
graphics at a very sophisticated level as well as the ability to store
this in digital form on a drive.

One of the key issues to keep in mind as we move more and more
toward graphics and high resolution bit-map displays is the ne-
cessity for high communications speeds to refresh the screens at
appropriate intervals. Another element seen in some offices today
is the HP-7475A, a 2- or 3-pin plotter available for under $1,000
and capable of doing excellent business graphics in work environments as a part of the local PC station.

Cynthia Peripherals.   A subsidiary of Honeywell, Cynthia Peripherals has been involved in Winchester disk technology, especially removable disk technologies. Winchester technology had
provided a very large volume storage capability—10 megabytes

or more. When those disk platters were full, however, the user had to buy a new one, an investment of $2,500 or more. We now have removable media. The cover of the Cynthia Peripherals device flops down and the user can pull out a 10-megabyte cartridge. This is perfect for things like electronic mail where files multiply like crazy. Now we can issue a 10-megabyte disk that has archival capabilities.

With such devices we have continued to off-load resources from the mainframe and even from the minicomputer. The result is that we now have a number of interesting capabilities at the local level. Such technology clearly requires a sophisticated management environment. We are moving toward a stage—probably near the end of the decade—in which data will be available in data banks at remote locations, artificial intelligence will be incorporated at the hardware level, and logic chips and wafer technology will permit the incredible capability of a 100 million instructions per second. From the user's perspective the key issue in this new stage is that the microcomputer becomes an extension of oneself, a transparent tool for the worker.

Trends in Personal Computer Software

*Mitchell Kapor**

The personal computer industry has, relatively speaking, no history. I've been involved with PCs since 1978, and that makes me an old-timer. In business personal computers became legitimate only a few years ago, with Visicalc on the Apple II. The first hardware legitimacy for personal computers in business came even more recently, with the IBM PC. Thus, to forecast what the industry may look like, what the products and their uses will be, is in my mind like looking at a first grader and determining what success in what profession that child is going to have.

Several characteristics of current product development and the computer field in general make the future uncertain. First it is important to note that the personal computer software products that have been most successful in the marketplace—Visicalc, dBase, Wordstar, and 1-2-3 are a few—were conceived of, inspired by, and developed through the efforts of single individuals or, at most, teams of two people working in isolation. In other words, those products came about through the heroic efforts of individual geniuses. Products developed through a more structured approach, which included a marketing requirements document and a formal development team—that is, products with good method-

*Mitchell Kapor is president of Lotus Development Corporation, Cambridge, Massachusetts.

28

ology—have not yet achieved the same degree of success in the marketplace. Two examples are Vision and Lisa; much is made of the hundreds of work-years that went into their development.

This is a significant fact for us at Lotus because we worry about how as an organization we are going to depend less on the efforts of individual geniuses. It is also a concern from a buyer's standpoint. If I were a data processing manager thinking about making a multimillion-dollar commitment to personal computers in my company, it would be important to deal with software vendors that had a track record in the marketplace. At present this is an unsolved problem.

To add fuel to the fire, the successful products I mentioned—1-2-3, dBase, Wordstar, and Visicalc—were all originally developed in assembly language. To my knowledge, the currently released versions still run in that language, which, for a number of reasons, gives much better performance. When you're dealing with limited resources performance in terms of speed and power is crucial, but such software is not very portable or responsive to the change in hardware environments. Successful commercial products for personal computers in a higher-level language, such as C or Pascal, have not yet been developed and in my view probably will not be accomplished with today's 16-bit technology. We will have to wait for 32-bit technology and go through our investigation again. In the 16-bit world you can make a better product—better in the sense of user acceptance—if you write it in assembly language. Portability and other assets are the trade-offs to make a product people will be happy with.

Another peculiarity of these successful products is that they were not developed out of any clear sense of market need. That is almost heresy. In the case of 1-2-3, for example, we looked at what was coming and said, "Aha, 16-bit technology is much better than 8-bit. We can do some important things." We looked at Visicalc and the other products and said, "It would be great if Visicalc had a graphing command in it." That was our market research.

This peculiar situation may stem from the fact that no one can be taught how to design a personal computer software product. It is possible to take courses, get degrees, go to seminars, and put together a huge bookshelf on how to write a compiler, how to do top-down structure systems design, and how to write transaction processing-oriented applications. There is training and a body of knowledge; there are experts and some well-recognized principles and practices. But none of these things tells you how to write a good productivity application for a personal computer. Writing such an application is an art as well as an exercise in trial and error; software designers are like medieval artisans. There is also a subjective and psychological element in the development of software products that please users. It involves recognizing what will feel right and what will work for the user. It's a big factor because end users are not programmers and are not necessarily comfortable with the technology.

Thus, software design is not the structured, orderly, systematic, rational, and controllable process that one would like to present to potential investors in a company's software technology. I assume that the training and the development of a design methodology will come in time, but it will be a long process.

I also know that more structured market research not only is possible but is already being done. In general, however, successful products still come about because someone has the germ of an idea and someone, either the same person or a different person, has the technological capability to begin working on that idea. They go off somewhere for six to nine months and come back with a product. That should make anyone nervous. For software companies such as Lotus or any of its competitors, long-term prospects depend on moving to another stage of development and implementation and even inspiration. We have a long way to go.

Besides the strongly individual and unpredictable nature of software design and development thus far, two other characteristics of the industry make forecasting difficult. The first is that software companies do not control their own destinies. Major software products are hardware-driven, which today means IBM-driven. The area of micro-to-mainframe communications is a good example of the kind of problem that affects Lotus and many other software companies. The market need is obviously there. PCs have to be hooked up, and we can see many possible approaches. Local area networks are one. Once you have 5, 10, 50, or 100 PCs handing off floppy disks from one user to the other soon becomes tiresome. If these users were connected in a local area network, they could share files and do electronic mail. In fact, organizations are already asking for these capabilities.

The software company, however, understandably wants to be cautious in implementing something that may have to be thrown out once IBM or another company announces something new.

Major hardware shifts upset everyone, and long-term prediction is quite difficult at this point. I can't say what we will be doing three years from now because I honestly don't know. I can only talk about what I think will happen in the next year.

A third characteristic that affects software forecasting is that nobody really understands what to do with a personal computer. We have this wonderful piece of technology for which creative people invent uses. The general public buys the tool because it does something for them on a day-to-day basis. But for our target market of managers and professionals I don't think the applications of personal computer technology will occupy more than 5 to 10 percent of their time. In the area of artificial intelligence, for example, I have given speeches about terrific products that could make managers and professionals more productive. But I don't know what shape such products might actually take or what their impact on end users or organizations might be because the creative spark for matching up the technology to market need is simply not there. You can't just hire a consultant to tell you, "Build this product." I have never seen a successful microcomputer product developed that way and I am quite pessimistic about such efforts.

So we are back to our small teams of heroic geniuses sitting in the corner. Even if they have a pipeline to a national corporate-user group, such as we have at Lotus, they simply cannot ask, "What do you want?" The technology is evolving so rapidly, both in hardware and software, that no one can fully articulate what is needed. An organization can only say, "Well, we think we need this, this, and this." But could any organization have said several years ago that what it specifically needed was Visicalc? Absolutely not. The idea for Visicalc came out of creator Dan Brickland's head, was realized as a product, and now has several million quite happy electronic spreadsheet users. Visicalc could not have been developed by going out and doing market research.

I expect the industry's long-term future to be very exciting, with innovative and useful applications being created and personal computers continuing to have a major impact in organizations. But I am quite uncertain about the nature of that impact and the kinds of developments that may occur beyond the next 12 months. Therefore, if it were my job to figure out what to do with personal computer technology in an organization, I would adopt a fairly cautious long-term approach. In the near term, however, we can say a number of things about what is likely to happen with software.

Recently some new buzzwords have emerged that offer some clues. One of them is "integrated software." What this says to me is that the ground rules are shifting and that the market expects IBM PCs or XTs to have available on them some multifunction application. Further, this multifunction application should address itself to a generic set of needs of users in organizations. There are five such broad application areas: spreadsheet, database, word processing, graphics, and communications. These needs are not new, but there is a much sharper focus and emphasis on new products coming out in these areas. Previously we had individual products such as Visicalc and Visiplot; today we have integrated offerings from Lotus, Visicorp, Apple with its Lisa machine, Context with its MBA package, and about 15 other companies.

It is apparent that, at least as a concept, integrated software is a big-win item. If you can deliver an integrated product that does several things well at an acceptable speed, that has a common command structure or user interface, and that has some ability to share data, you are removing a lot of the fragmentation that existed previously with individual products. If by learning one set of commands you can access database data in a spreadsheet, make graphs from a spreadsheet, and incorporate pieces of the database into your word processor, you have a much more versatile product.

There seems to be general agreement that the five applications—spreadsheet, database, word processing, graphics, and communication—while not exhaustive, answer basic productivity needs. Beyond that, there is a diversity of approaches being taken toward integrated software. No one has yet delivered the perfect product, which, I think, would have to perform the five individual applications quite well. In other words, if you give people a spreadsheet application so they can do their forecasting or their planning it has to be at least as good as stand-alone spreadsheets. Similarly, a word processing application that will be used for everything from dashing off a quick memo to doing a complete report or document should not be a substantial compromise below a stand-alone word processor.

The inevitability of some compromise is one of the many criticisms of integrated software packages, but I believe the geniuses will solve that particular problem, as they have others. They will do so because you cannot expect people to accept a product that forces them to give up features, convenience, power, or anything else they are used to. They won't buy it, they won't use it, and it will sit on the shelf.

Simply meeting application needs, however, is insufficient. There is further agreement, I think, that integrated products as application have to be open-ended so that they can connect in different ways to other applications, to vertical market products, to mainframes, to minicomputers, to voice. But there is no general agreement about the best type of open system. We will continue to see diversity until the market votes with its dollars.

I would like to focus on the prospects for two broad approaches to integrated software. The first is the integration of the applications themselves. Recently, what I call the window-mouse type of system, both in the Apple Lisa and the Vision product, received a great deal of attention. Quite a few other products adopted that metaphor. With this system it is possible to create different windows or physical regions on a screen, each of which can have a different application in it. As a user I can set up my system so that I have my word processing in one window and my database in another. I can blow up a single window and work with a full-screen spreadsheet, then shrink it back down. And I control the entire application using a pointing device such as a mouse. The general enthusiasm for the window approach, particularly with the mouse, appears to be leveling off. There has even been some mouse backlash claiming that perhaps keyboards are not so bad after all, especially for creating a document.

For me, the main problem of the window approach is that there are different applications in each window. These are like little islands connected by bridges over which data move. Let me give a concrete example using Lisacalc, which is a spreadsheet: To do forecasts and graphs, you have to cut the data out of the window and put it onto a clipboard. It then gets pasted into the graphing program and makes a graph. To change a number on the spreadsheet or to get different summary numbers, you must move back to the spreadsheet window, enter the new number, cut the data out and paste it back in again. This turns out to be a laborious and cumbersome process.

What people really want is to make some new numbers, hit a key, and see a new graph come up on the screen. No one has yet discovered how to do this in a window system. Each window (application) has its own separate data structure sharing a common interface so that things can be moved around. But from the user's point of view, why is this necessary? Why can't the user have a unitary data structure that can be called up as a document, or a spreadsheet, or a database? Although this might be a much more satisfactory approach for the users, it has yet to be realized. So it is back into the little locked room for the geniuses to design a viable product based on user need.

The second approach to integrated software and, I think, the big coup, has to do with the integration of data rather than the integration of the user interface. Things should be simple, straightforward, consistent, and intuitive for users. A common user interface certainly goes a long way toward that goal, but until data is completely transparent to the user, many people will shy away from using the products.

This integration of data is involved not only in the personal computer but is also important in the micro-to-mainframe link. We are in the midst of a great deal of very painful progress in that area. Recent developments are certainly making it much easier and more convenient to move data from a mainframe to a personal computer, but we are still at a rather primitive stage in terms of how we actually put the data inside of a PC. The process will not be transparent until the next generation in development, whenever that occurs.

There is also a long way to go in the area of communications. I predict that it will be people in organizations willing to invest and devote more of their own resources and cleverness who will develop usable systems. And I expect it will take a least another couple of years to see this happen.

I have no doubt that we are going to see good integrated applications and integrated data structure. But I think it is equally important that future software products be as open-ended as possible and have different qualities or types of open-endedness. In the near future, I think it is safe to say that organizations may have their own staffs of application developers. They will want to create custom applications for their own corporate needs or they may wish to create applications in some vertical market and sell them. Organizations may want either to develop an application from scratch or some higher-level language that talks to integrated applications so users can get the benefit of the spreadsheet, the graphing, and the database regardless of the specific application.

Beyond development from scratch, which is expensive, time consuming, and hard to control, a productivity application can be made open-ended so that an expert user (not a programmer) within the organization can create a model template application. This application can then be used as a standard within the organization. To do this, however, expert users must have the necessary tools. The first, stumbling effort Lotus made in this direction was to include a macrolanguage with 1-2-3 that contained the rudiments of a formal programming language, control structures, variables assignments, and user interface primitives. It is clumsy and anything but elegant, but it is being used in corporations far more than we ever could have predicted. In fact, some of our corporate accounts have devoted 5 and 10 work-years of development in this area and their results are being distributed to hundreds, perhaps thousands, of users within their own organizations worldwide.

A third type of open-endedness allows the individual application to talk to and work with other off-the-shelf retail applications. I predict that in the future usage patterns may well be focused on one or two core standardized products within the organization. At the same time there will be legitimate needs for perhaps as many as two dozen other more specific applications that can also be purchased off the shelf. Therefore, it is critical that a core productivity application be able to be integrated with those other applications. There are a variety of approaches that will be coming out to achieve this.

In sum, open-endedness is not a simple thing. There are communities of users with different needs, vertical market needs, internal needs, the desire to create salable add-on applications to a core product. I think it will take a couple of years to sort out what the most desired aspects of open-endedness are and to determine what will become the accepted standard.

Blessing or curse, we live in interesting times. Despite all the uncertainties I am quite optimistic about the value of delivering personal computer software and in particular integrated software. I see an absolute shift in these deliveries toward the corporate marketplace. As this shift is taking place, I think software companies are maturing as entrepreneurs and are learning to understand the real needs of organizations. With a modest amount of patience on both sides, organizations and computer companies are going to achieve their mutual goal of delivering good information processing to the broadest community of users.

Personal Computer Networks

*Robert M. Metcalfe**

There are three kinds of people in the world: the technologists who believe that technology can, will, and should turn the world upside down and who are engaged principally in revolution; the users who believe that everything is moving too quickly, wish it were 1965 again, and whose principal activity is counterinsurgency; and those who recognize that technology will reach useful application more slowly than most technologists would like and more quickly than most users would like. The progress of this technology is measured not by any absolute timeframe, but on the basis of how successful we are in matching the superstructure of technology to the infrastructure of organizations.

Local networking, for example, is one technology whose superstructure is now being matched, successfully, to the infrastructures of various organizations. It is a technology bent on revolution: in my view, the next decade can be characterized from a computing standpoint as the decade of the local networking of personal computers. This represents the third major phase in the history of computers and in the application of computing technology. Not long ago computing meant batch processing on main-

---

*Robert M. Metcalfe is founder, chairman, and vice-president of strategies and projects, 3Com Corporation, Mountain View, California.

frames—the first phase. Then computing became timesharing on minicomputers—the second phase. Now we are moving more and more into local networking of personal computers. Each phase broadens the market for computing and the number of applications for computing and brings more and more computing to a greater number of people.

Networking adds a sixth category to Mitchell Kapor's five applications—word processing, spreadsheet, database, graphics, and communications. What are variously called local computer networks, local area networks, or more frequently just networking answer the need for a system to connect hundreds of computers on separate desks. There are approximately 200 varieties of local networks now being sold, of which Ethernet is only one.

There are two approaches to this third stage of computer development: what I call the ethercentric view and the boxcentric view. It is easy to identify which is which. Ask people to draw their computer systems on the blackboard. If they begin by drawing a box they are boxcentric. If they begin by drawing a sweeping line across the board they are ethercentric and have adopted the revolutionary view that communication is central. Computers are viewed as the array of resources around communication; they are seen less as arithmetic devices and more as communication tools.

With the arrival of personal computers—particularly the IBM PC—in large enough numbers and with sufficient power to be usefully connected at high speed in local networks, the pressures for the development of networking became overwhelming. Now that the IBM PC is here, many believe that all progress can stop. I do not subscribe to that point of view; I do believe that many other personal computers will continue the trend toward increased computer power on the desk. But the important crossover has already occurred between the cost of providing multimegabit, high-speed local networking, as represented by Ethernet, and the density and power of personal computers. This means that it is now important enough and cheap enough for a small portion of the industry to get involved in networking personal computers. So the ceiling tiles are coming down again and more cables are going in.

For what are these local networks of personal computers being used? First there are the basics, such as peripheral sharing. With more and more personal computers economics becomes increasingly important. Sharing resources, principally printers and disks, is the first step. We start out by trying to do what we are already doing more cheaply. We then try to do things we haven't done before, which begins the second phase of local networking.

This second phase involves the use of local networks to give access to personal computers or to give personal computers access to information. Most of the information currently computerized is on mainframes. Thus, a high-priority item is to give personal computers access to mainframes. That is why the IBM PC 3270, which allows PCs to act as terminals and get information that already exists on mainframes, is so significant. As less and less of our information exists on mainframes, however, the priority will shift to personal computers communicating with each other. Now that personal computers exist, there is a trend to bring data into the local workgroup where they are generated and used. In the future, I believe we will see as much as 80 percent of the computerized data being kept not on a corporate mainframe but on a departmental or even a workgroup-shared file system.

The third and final use of local networks of personal computers is as tools for communications. This brings up the subject of electronic mail.

In 1970 the appeal of electronic mail was that you didn't have to move paper around anymore—you could move electrons. And the transmission of electrons was much less expensive than the transmission of cellulose. It appeared that electronic mail was concerned with transmission, moving information, and the economies of moving electronic information. However, we quickly realized that although the cost of sending the information might be low we were spending 15 dollars to prepare the document we were sending. Electronic mail was synonymous with its preparation, and it became very preparation-intensive.

We also realized that we were spending a lot of time moving electronic mail from desk to desk manually after computers prepared and transmitted it. The fact is, most people don't want to send messages from one post office to another, they want to send them from one desk to another. Electronic mail then became a distribution problem—specifically the development and maintenance of distribution lists. We are now in the distribution phase of this trend in personal communication. The focus of current progress is the creation of distribution mechanisms for electronic mail. And the computer industry is moving into the next phase.

Because local networks of personal computers are so effective at generating and delivering electronic messages, electronic mail has become a filing and database problem. We now receive so many important messages we can't afford to throw away the 10 megabytes that can be quickly consumed by our electronic correspondence. In the future, electronic mail will involve even more data-intensive modes—for example, voice integration in the messaging system, eliminating the telephone tag but maintaining voice, and eventually forms-base messaging in which the contents of the message is machine processable.

Where does software development fit into the trend toward local networking of personal computers? I would put software into five broad categories in terms of its relation to networking. In some of these categories actual software does not yet exist. The first category I would call "unnetworked" software, and there is little of it left. Unnetworked software runs only on a personal computer and cannot in any way be networked, either because there is no transparent networking available or because the software implementors have not used the standard operating system available. Very few of these software packages would interest organizations.

The second category can be called transparently networked software. This is software that uses the operating system cleanly, and networking facilities that have been developed for that operating system can be used transparently by preexisting software. Most of the software that is available today, including 1-2-3, can be and is transparently networked.

The third category I refer to as network-delivered software. The use of the network to deliver the software is a substitute for the floppy disks that most of us have come to think of as a delivery mechanism for software. Examples are Visicalc and Visiword that can now be distributed without diskettes through 3Com's local network. These facilities can be bought for a large group of users. Supply users with the appropriate number of manuals, and they can get that software over the network much more quickly than they can off a floppy disk. And, they do not have to worry about storing the floppy disk. Those of us who were involved in the struggle to eliminate punch cards during the 1970s are now in the process of eliminating floppy disks.

The fourth category of software I call multiaccess (or multiuser) networked software. The best example of this would be a dBase II personal computer database package that would allow users on multiple PCs to be concurrently accessing and updating a shared database through the network. This is not the same as transparent networking using the current dBase, which is a single-user system that does not provide for shared access to the same database. With such a system, there is the danger of multiple accesses damaging each other. Thus, the obvious next step is making available multiaccess database software using local networks to bring a number of PC users to the same database for concurrent access and update.

The fifth and final category I call network-integrated software. Just as in 1-2-3, which integrates database, word processing, and graphics into a uniform user interface, and just as in Vision, where the entire user interface has been integrated along with a variety of applications, we can think of integrating networking into other applications for volume management. The movement of data from one place to another is a part of the natural use of integrated applications.

As far as I know, only the first three software categories now exist: unnetworked, transparently networked, and network-delivered. But the other two are coming. In fact, the objective of the fifth category of software is to eliminate itself. In other words, when networking software exists, we won't have to talk about it as a separate category because it will be lost in the integration and become part of the applications that users actually need. No one actually needs networking, they need the applications it makes possible. These applications will be the focus of the coming decade.

PART II
SMALL COMPUTERS IN LARGE ORGANIZATIONS
The Implications

Introduction

*Hannah I. Blank**

The implications of small computer technology for large organizations, whether corporate, government, or academic, are far-reaching. They include technical, organizational, and, to some extent, societal issues.

The technical implications may be the least difficult to handle:

• Data processing (DP) professionals will need new skills, such as interfacing micros with minis or mainframes and generating applications from generic packages with programmer tools different from what they are accustomed to using.

• Questions of architecture will have to be solved. Where does the microcomputer fit in the overall computer architecture of a given organization?

• Data integrity and security are high-visibility concerns magnified by the ubiquity of the micro and the ease with which diskettes can be copied and transported.

Small computer technology has generated a new set of implications for an organization and its management:

• New job descriptions are emerging. Functions that did not exist before are to some extent replacing existing functions.

• Higher skills may be required in the same job functions. This may appear threatening to some individuals, while others may regard it as an opportunity. One example is the use of the micro-

---

*Hannah I. Blank is vice-president of the Domestic Institutional Bank, Chase Manhattan Bank, New York, New York.

computer by the secretary not only for word processing but for functions related to spreadsheets, data management, and even graphics. Some may respond enthusiastically to learning new skills; others may be intimidated.

• Different loci of power are being created in the organization, and turf issues abound.

• Motivated by their own productivity needs, people outside the data processing field, such as financial analysts, are to some extent directing the use of micros. This can pose a threat to the control that DP management has regarded as its right and responsibility.

A whole range of societal implications and concerns are inevitable as microcomputers become a part of our everyday lives:

• Unlike the mainframe and the minicomputer, whose use was confined to a professional class with specialized skills, the microcomputer is infiltrating the lives of a great many people. It is accessible and usable at some level of complexity by virtually everyone. On the job this will increase the demand for micros, for training, and for mobility. It also means that some computer literacy will in all likelihood be acquired at home.

• The microcomputer adds fuel to the flames over "homework," an emotional issue for women and minorities. Homework has positive benefits for women with children who do not want to leave home for a full working day; for the disabled who cannot leave home; and for individuals with many interests who wish to work only part time. Posed against these benefits are the opportunities for employee exploitation on the part of the employers. The cost and transportability of the micro magnify the possibilities.

The next three chapters offer a closer look at some of the specific problems that are arising as microcomputers become accepted tools in large organizations.

John Bennett, of United Technologies Corporation, considers the implications of microcomputer growth for both systems departments and general management. Ray Kline, of the General Services Administration, explains some of the problems the federal government faces and the steps it is taking to respond to technological change while maintaining management control. Finally, James H. Bair, of Hewlett-Packard, explores the evolution of microcomputers and their potential roles in the office of the future.

Managing Uncontrollable Growth

John H. Bennett*

The explosion in the acquisition and use of minicomputers and microcomputers is by now quite familiar. Over the past 10 years I have observed this growth from the point of view of a large, diversified, multinational corporation, United Technologies Corporation (UTC).

United Technologies is a Fortune 100 corporation whose companies manufacture many kinds of high technology products. These include Pratt & Whitney Aircraft engines, Sikorsky helicopters, Carrier air-conditioning systems, Otis elevators, Mostek semiconductors, and a broad range of electrical and electronic devices and controls. All of these companies are experiencing the current microcomputer revolution. Since UTC allows its divisions a high degree of autonomy in management, each has reacted in its own way, both to the pressures of technological change and to the guidelines provided by the corporate office. Thus, UTC offers a unique opportunity to study a variety of companies, determine what the major common problems are, and see what managerial responses seem to be most successful.

Most organizations using computer technology experience growth in the number of terminals used. While this growth rate is

*John H. Bennett is corporate director of data processing for United Technologies Corporation, Hartford, Connecticut.

steady, it is by and large related to the rate of installation of systems on a central computer. Thus, it is nominally under control. Workstation growth is a different story.

Proceeding from a smaller base, word processors, personal computers, engineering design stations, and intelligent remote job-entry stations are growing at a much faster rate. Many of these applications require little or no immediate support from an organization's main data center. The systems are inexpensive enough to get over or around the hurdles of cost justification that corporate bureaucracies have placed in the path of computer acquisition. Their growth is thus difficult to control. However, management of the process is obviously necessary for a couple of reasons. Many applications will eventually require data access and data integrity; others clearly should be carried out on a central computer.

The reasons for this rapid growth are threefold: service, economics, and control. Most computer service organizations or departments have a backlog of up to two years of cost-justified applications. Customers see minicomputers and microcomputers as a shortcut around this bottleneck. Their cost is relatively easy to justify, and users have at least the appearance of being in control of their own destiny.

The impact of these developments on computer service organizations has been devastating. The first symptoms of change took the systems departments by surprise. User departments presented requests for special-purpose, minicomputer-based terminal systems for special applications. The first requests seemed innocuous enough: a computer for a laboratory; a dedicated test application; a stand-alone, computer-aided drafting application. Such projects were outside the normal range of competence or responsibility of most data processing departments, and they were clearly limited in scope. Or were they?

At United Technologies over 500 of the Digital Equipment Corporation PDP 11s have now been brought in for these "limited" applications. There are over 50 VAXs with their full network of supported terminals, virtually all of which are beyond the direct control of the systems department. The same drama is about to be played out in the area of manufacturing support.

The first microcomputers were brought into my corporation by their owners, who were convinced of their utility but could not get approval to purchase them. In one division I found that an employee had set up his own micro in a conference room and provided a sign-up sheet so that other employees could schedule time to use it. Needless to say, I felt obligated to mention to management that an Apple computer is far too inexpensive to have expensive professional employees queueing up for it.

Now, of course, the problem has changed to one of moderating the rate of acquisition. For the first time computer service organizations are being threatened by their own technologies. The warnings are clear: Improve service or lose control. A two-year backlog is no longer viable. The IBM solution is not the only acceptable one. And corporate data can no longer be accessible only to information specialists.

The two-year backlog is, of course, the result of a rational attempt to establish priorities for a large workload. An unfortunate consequence is that small jobs, important only to one person or one department, never seem to get done. A number of options are available to computer service organizations (CSOs) to attack this backlog. System generators and application generators are one obvious choice. These tools can make a programmer up to five times more effective. Such tools also tend to be self-documenting, making later maintenance easier.

Another tool-related problem has been the willingness of some departments to sacrifice service to the user in favor of operational convenience. Many CSO managers who have pointed to IBM or some other preferred vendor's solution to a problem as if it were the only solution are now waking up to find their customers installing another vendor's equipment and running proprietary software. And in the process their own responsibilities have been reduced to downloading data files to the new system. More enlightened departments have tried to provide modern tools for users to get at their data.

Some CSOs have even taken the offensive and initiated education programs to show users what systems can do for them, including what approaches are likely to be successful and what the limitations are. These programs may be addressed to a specific group, such as a manufacturing unit, or to management in general. Such efforts improve the odds that whatever approach a user decides on—mini, micro, or main computer—will be reasonable and will have a high chance for success.

Microcomputer growth has produced a number of problems for general management as well as for systems departments. The problem of computer security, both external and internal, is now a concern at the highest levels of corporate management. With more managers and executives using terminals and personal computers, the problems of data access and corresponding data security can no longer be avoided. UTC is only one of many companies considering new guidelines for computer security.

Cost is another management problem. In more and more corporate negotiations over system support, service wins out over compatibility. Terminal-based systems are more expensive than their batch report counterparts, whether they are mini, micro, or main computer based. At UTC, for example, the cost of hardware is growing both in absolute dollars and as a percentage of the data processing budget, despite the advancing technology.

United Technologies Corporation has used a number of approaches to manage the latest stage of the computer revolution. The most obvious is the use of report writers and other high-level languages. These allow data processing professionals to respond to requests for service that require occasional reports drawn from existing data bases or the calculation of specific results on an infrequent basis. Some of these tools are simple enough to be taught to end users as well.

Along with the personal computer, these new tools are the major focus of the information centers that are currently springing up throughout United Technologies. The information center at the Essex Group Headquarters, for example, has achieved national acclaim. It uses terminals, microcomputers, and user-friendly software to help its customers perform a variety of tasks that might otherwise have to be done by data processing.

Another response to service problems is to tackle the backlog directly by increasing programmer productivity. There is increased interest today in the use of automated programming aids such as program generators. In the area of program or system generators UTC has been somewhat conservative. The Raytheon product, Readi-Code, is used at one company; the Burroughs product, LINK, is used at another; a third unit using a home-grown applications generator is probably the best of the three. I cannot overemphasize the power of a well-designed application generator. One of UTC's smaller divisions installed a broad range of financial and administrative systems over a two-and-one-half-year period. During that time the systems development group never included more than two-and-one-half employees. All applications were fully customized, not packages. The latest was a complex purchasing system (10,000 lines of COBOL code) begun in May and turned over to the users for testing in August.

UTC is perhaps unique in the area of management education. In 1982 the company decided to invest in a major effort to educate its executives in the capabilities of computers. The method chosen was to develop a training program for executives. The resulting program, implemented in late 1982, is called the Executive Personal Computing Workshop. This workshop, a three-day session conducted at the United Technologies Research Center, is restricted to senior managers and executives. It offers a hands-on approach using the IBM personal computer and the Context MBA software. Following the program, participants receive a personal computer for their "business use."

Executives in this program are taught to use an array of standard tools: automated spreadsheets, word processing, business graphics, and communications. No job-specific applications or programming techniques are taught. Although the three-day time period does not permit inclusion of database applications, a self-study database module has been developed for later study. Considerable effort was spent developing this program, which includes custom training materials rather than manuals. Individual workstations are connected to the instructor's station through a switching network that allows participants to view the instructor's screen on their own screens by flipping a switch. The program has been well accepted and is one of the most popular the corporation has ever run. It suggests the type of imagination that data processing organizations will need in the future if they are to regain control of their enterprise.

The current upheaval has some predictable longer-term effects as well. First, it is safe to assume that by the end of the decade virtually every white-collar worker, and many others, will have or have access to some form of workstation. The intelligence built onto that station will vary with user need. Similarly, whether it is connected to a minicomputer or a mainframe will depend on the application. Second, this rapid growth in workstations will impose an enormous training requirement on organizations. Already companies are springing up to meet this need, and vendors are unbundling their training to reap additional profit. Even computer service organizations will not be immune to this training requirement due to the acquisition of new productivity tools.

What will happen to computer service departments in the future? Clearly there will be far less need for mundane programming skills given the use of productivity tools both by the systems department and by customers. Although computers will be much more widely distributed than they are today, systems departments will neither wither away nor will their leaders become super information executives. On the contrary, these departments will return to their original function of providing professional services consisting of computer support, file management, systems analysis, and program generation. They will be smaller, highly professional organizations.

Finally, if our organizations have an apparent destiny, we must decide how we can best lead them toward it. There are two sides to this question, which can be illustrated by two stories.

The first story is about the traveling salesman who, after searching several hours for his destination, finally encounters a farmer. When asked how to reach the destination, the farmer sadly replies, "You can't get there from here." Luckily, for most of us, the situation is not that bad. For some companies, however, that statement is all too true. Faced with fragmented systems responsibilities, internal bickering over resources, and no central control or management commitment, the only way they can deal with the coming changes is to restructure, to become different organizations.

The second story comes from Lewis Carroll's classic, *Alice's Adventures in Wonderland*. Alice, who is lost, asks one of the consultants of her day, the Cheshire Cat, for directions:

> "Would you tell me, please, which way I ought to go from here?"
> "That depends a good deal on where you want to get to," said the Cat.
> "I don't much care where—" said Alice.
> "Then it doesn't matter which way you go," said the Cat.
> "—so long as I get *somewhere*," added Alice, as an explanation.
> "Oh, you're sure to do that," said the Cat, "if you only walk long enough."

This exchange reflects the more normal situation in many companies now trying to make decisions about which way to go with computer technology. The possible paths are management approaches. The goals—where we want to go—are strategic directions. We must choose:

• Do we want to be on the leading edge of the technology and possibly achieve a strategic advantage over our competitors? If so, the cost is high, and so is the risk of costly blunders. We have to develop many of our own tools. Cost-benefit analysis as a management tool is virtually useless.

- Are we willing to stay a step behind the leading edge? If so, we are less likely to achieve a competitive advantage. However, the cost is less and so is the risk. Most applications can be economically justified. But some decisions will still have to be justified on strategic grounds.

- Do we want to stay well back from the leading edge, implementing only proven and therefore cost-effective systems changes? If so, we will have minimum cost and minimum risk of failure. We are, however, at maximum risk of finding ourselves at a competitive disadvantage.

I cannot recommend which path to take. Each company must make its own choice, and it should choose a path consistent with its management approach in other areas. But most importantly, it should not pick a path by default and it should not let its technicians do the choosing.

Managed Innovation
Controlling End-User Computing in the Federal Government
Ray Kline*

In 1982 the General Services Administration (GSA), responding to the long-awaited microcomputer revolution, convened a small group of knowledgeable people in government to help determine what the federal government's policies should be in this emerging area. The group met every two or three weeks to look at various aspects of the problem and to see what might be done. The quandary it faced was change versus control—the government's need to be responsive to technological change and the need to maintain management control.

In the area of computer technology, of course, change is essential and inevitable. Decades ago the federal government was in the vanguard of automated data processing and related technologies. Today it lags behind. Studies during the Ford administration (1974–1976) placed government about 10 years behind the private sector. By 1983 the Grace Commission reported that the gap was only 6.7 years. It is possible that by 1990 we will have caught up with or even surpassed the private sector. However, the driving force to initiate change is not merely to keep up with the private sector but to improve the efficiency of government and to increase the productivity of the federal worker. President Reagan has impressed upon his entire cabinet the need to cut gov-

---

*Ray Kline is acting administrator of the U.S. General Services Administration.

ernment spending, to increase productivity dramatically, and to perform the functions of government at a lower cost with fewer people.

At the same time there is the need to maintain control. And in the federal bureaucracy controls are imposed somewhat differently than in the private sector. The government is not, as one often reads, just another large corporation. There is a General Accounting Office (GAO), congressional legislation, a board of directors (Congress) not always in agreement with the chief executive officer (the President). All of these players must be considered when developing effective controls for microcomputers in the federal government.

Compounding the problem, the GAO has issued an audit report stating that a runaway condition exists in the use of personal computers in the federal bureaucracy. This situation has arisen even sooner than originally predicted. Federal employees aren't waiting for guidance. They are bringing in their own equipment and putting it to work. In my trips around the country I have seen the growing number of computers, and although the numbers vary in different departments no one can deny that there is a lot of activity. In the budget for fiscal year 1985, for example, new automation requirements are in the hundreds of millions of dollars. These requirements serve to indicate what employees want to do with personal computers as well as with some of the larger systems. Some degree of control in this process is imperative.

With these two considerations in mind—the need to make change and the need to control it—GSA's microcomputer assessment group performed its work and in June 1983 released a report, *Managing End-User Computing in the Federal Government*. The assessment group identified three components of end-user computing: mode, users, and technologies (Table 1).

From a management perspective the report concludes that the integrated mode requires the most attention. In reviewing users and technologies the assessment group observed that in the past heavy emphasis was placed on clerical applications. Now the technology has useful applications throughout the work force. Therefore, although the group focused on personal computers, other technologies were considered, along with the broad range of potential users.

The group considered two possible courses of action to deal with the growth of personal computers in the federal government.

TABLE 1   Components of End-User Computing

Mode	Technologies	Users
Stand-alone	Word processing	Clericals
Integrated	Optical character recognition	Office professionals
	Electronic mail	Scientists
	Micrographics	
	Facsimile	
	Personal computers	
	Dictation systems	
	Terminals and networks	
	Document storage/retrieval	
	Graphics	
	Distribution data processing	

One was to institute a moratorium on the purchase of computers until things could be sorted out. The other was to allow activity to continue and try to provide an interim environment for learning. Needless to say, judgment ran in favor of the latter.

The group then began to look at what kinds and levels of controls and supports would be helpful in creating this learning environment. In the process members of GSA's Advisory Board, composed mainly of vice-presidents of private sector companies, were asked about the controls they imposed on their own end-user computing. Approximately half said they had tight controls. The other half said they had rather loose controls, and some wished they could begin again and include more control features.

The assessment group began to shape a new microcomputer management environment around the idea of sticks and carrots. Control was the stick; support or encouragement was the carrot. Sticks include the kinds of standards that should be imposed on people and organizations and the levels at which such restrictions apply. The group identified three main types of carrots—procurement vehicles, support structures, and education tools. In each area the group concluded that more and better carrots were needed. For example, there was room for much improvement and streamlining of the federal procurement system. Support structures in departments and agencies were not at the levels they should be. Improvement was needed in both managerial support of changes and technical support to new users. More and better education tools were required at all levels. The most obvious needs in the education area were for better training plans, reference tools such as buyer's guides, and a clearinghouse for information on what other people were doing.

From a broad perspective, what was needed during this transitional learning period was an environment for growth at a pace in keeping with each organization's ability to effectively apply a new technology. The assessment group evolved several broad goals to underlie its management recommendations for this transition period:

- Create a friendly but well-managed environment.
- Don't scare people with too many control systems.
- Encourage the use of technology to improve productivity. Improved productivity must be the end result because, without the private sector's bottom line, productivity is the only way to judge whether efforts are truly cost-effective. Beware of the runaway train syndrome, which could result one day in a pile of unproductive equipment and a situation that is out of control.

The group called its approach the "managed innovation program." Its objective was to meet the needs of a one- or two-year transition period. During this time microcomputer users could develop an understanding of what is going on in the marketplace, and the market itself might stabilize somewhat. There are two parts to the managed innovation program: a set of 13 governmentwide initiatives for which GSA is responsible and 12 individual agency initiatives. These initiatives are summarized in Table 2.

Governmentwide initiatives fall into four categories of purpose: policy, agency assistance, education, and in-house learning. These served as common denominators for the recommendations and suggestions made by the assessment group.

The group had to evolve policy not for the long term, but for the transition period. Thus, it recognized the need for a fact-finding facility to stay current with the activities of different departments and agencies, many of which were quite advanced. Local data-network policy was another area that needed consideration. An interagency group is now working to develop a deeper understanding in this area that may evolve into policy guidelines. A final policy area involved revision of the regulations and the

TABLE 2 GSA's Managed Innovation Program Initiatives—Governmentwide and Within Agencies

Governmentwide		Individual Agency	
Purpose	Initiative	Purpose	Initiative
Policy	1. Develop a fact-finding facility. 2. Develop a local data network policy. 3. Revise regulations and guidelines.	Policy and planning	1. Establish a general policy. 2. Develop a strategic plan. 3. Develop agencywide data rules. 4. Consider a telecommunications network. 5. Use standards to promote compatibility.
Agency assistance	4. Develop a buyer's guide. 5. Develop a procedures cookbook. 6. Provide procurement vehicles for equipment and software. 7. Develop a nationwide cluster maintenance contract.	Review	6. Establish an evaluation program.
		Process	7. Develop concise justification procedures. 8. Establish review and approval procedures.
Education	8. Organize a conference for agency executives. 9. Establish a forum for line managers in agencies. 10. Promote a joint literacy plan.	Use assistance	9. Identify classes of uses and users. 10. Encourage formation of tribes. 11. Establish support structures.
In-house learning	11. Investigate questions of records management. 12. Conduct a data and equipment compatibility project. 13. Perform an end-user pilot project.	Education	12. Develop a computer-literacy plan.

guidelines themselves to make them more responsive to actual needs.

Governmentwide initiatives should help people get started. The managed innovation program calls for agency assistance in two main areas. One involves obtaining and maintaining equipment, providing procurement vehicles for equipment and software and developing a nationwide cluster maintenance contract to streamline procurement modes. The other involves helping the user by providing buying and procedural guides.

Governmentwide initiatives have already begun in the area of education. In 1983 senior executives from federal agencies met to discuss problems and make suggestions about how GSA could improve its central management performance and about what individual agencies could do.

In the area of in-house learning there have been some notable achievements within individual agencies, such as the Department of Agriculture's graduate school program, the GSA Interagency Training Center, and other departmental efforts. New initiatives are needed. GSA conducted its own end-user pilot project, one of the recommended initiatives in the in-house learning category.

Initiatives of individual agencies form the second part of the managed innovation program. Although specifics will differ according to the needs of each agency or department, initiatives can be grouped in four broad areas: policy and planning review, process, use assistance, and education.

In the policy and planning area the top management of each agency must assume responsibility. Further, the organization needs to understand top management's position on microcomputers to move through the transition phase and into the future. Strategic planning for microcomputers should address both vertical (top-down) and horizontal perspectives on the organization.

Planning must also take into account the need for agencywide data regulations and periodic reviews to determine that resources are being used properly. Management must make sure that the public's money is being well spent. Agencies must move away from the earlier management mentality, which was dominated by the large, mainframe, automatic data processing departments. They must avoid the trap of believing that the only way to control the end-user computing environment is to employ the kind of controls imposed on the large systems in the 1960s. In its report the assessment group recommends that computing be placed in the hands of line managers, giving them the resources they need to do their particular jobs.

In the areas of user assistance and education recommended initiatives include encouraging people with common problems to get together, providing ways to help them, and developing computer-literacy plans that meet individual and agency needs.

After the assessment group completed its report GSA began to apply its principles through an end-user pilot project. Top management informed GSA's 30,000 employees around the country that it was interested in their ideas on end-user computing. To evaluate the end-user computing proposals that resulted, the agency formed a two-person review panel made up of one member who understood the world of end-user computing and the other who understood the breadth of GSA's activities. Proposals had to include justifications not exceeding one page, a brief description of the application, and an estimate of the gain in productivity. GSA received over 100 proposals, and about half were approved. The people involved in the proposals that have been implemented are convinced of the value of these tools to the performance of their jobs. To help them use the approved applications, GSA set up a three-member technical support group. The agency also set up a steering committee and authorized some broader applications throughout the organization, such as automating many of the General Counsel's activities and tying in with the White House's system of electronic mail.

The end-user pilot project has resulted in some real improvements. There has been a definite gain in productivity. Reports are coming out in a fraction of the time that had previously been required. Capabilities now exist for "what-if" analysis that were not previously available. Finally, the quality and accuracy of the work product have improved.

Perhaps just as important, the project also identified areas that need more attention. Proposal ideas came, by and large, from people directly involved with end-user applications, and reflected their considerable knowledge. But the proposals also reflected the fact that people had obviously been working and learning pretty much on their own. They pointed up the need for a strong, effective training component, including a survey course of what an end-user computer can do and a hands-on training session. The agency concluded that, in terms of training time, there should be at least a two-to-one ratio of hands-on training versus lecture. To limit training to broad brush exposure is not enough. All 50 people involved in the pilot project stressed the need for much more initial hands-on training in order to achieve competency in a much shorter period of time.

In the area of technical support GSA found it indispensable to have an in-house group of people who are not vendors to advise and help users by answering questions, many of them procedural, on how to get things going. Such in-house capability eliminates the problem of a vendor walking off after delivering equipment or software and leaving users to their own devices as problems arise.

In the area of procurement GSA found some isolated cases in which computers were being chosen on the basis of price alone, with no consideration for training and support components. In certain cases the hardware came from vendors hundreds of miles away, making on-site support extremely difficult. Such experiences emphasized the importance of procurement procedures that focus not merely on the hardware price alone, but include the total package of hardware, software, training, and technical support.

GSA is now applying the knowledge gained from the pilot project to its microcomputer management system. The agency has also moved into requirements contracting to cover its end-user computing needs. GSA learned through this end-user computing experiment that there are four or five applications that cover 85 percent of the needs. The requirements package being provided for the acquisition of hardware will meet the needs of those predominant applications.

GSA has made considerable progress in dealing with the problems of end-user computing in the federal government. However, there is still much to learn. Looking to the future, the agency expects the current initiatives of the managed innovation program to evolve into a management pattern that will benefit the federal government and ultimately the taxpayer in a cost-effective way.

Personal Computers and the Office of the Future

*James H. Bair**

A historical perspective is helpful in understanding where small computer technology is headed. In the beginning, back in 1945, Vannevar Bush proposed that computers could serve as an extension to human memory. That idea took shape at Stanford Research Institute in the early 1960s as an augmented human intellect system. This system in turn evolved into augmented knowledge workshops and eventually into the concept of office automation, a system that was actually demonstrated at the National Computer Conference in 1967.

The "office of the future," as it was conceived then, never really got off the ground. It was generally superseded by personal computers. But some of the issues that were typical then are still important today and will continue to be issues as we move toward integrating the personal computer into the mainstream of digital technology.

One way to look at evolution—in this case, the evolution of digital technology—is in terms of the "share of mind" that a technology commands at a given time. In fact, it is not really the technology but some manifestation of it that has the share of mind.

Prior to 1960 scientific and military computing was the dominant manifestation. Then, management information systems

---

*James H. Bair is manager of advanced systems for the Information Systems Group, Hewlett-Packard Co., Cupertino, California.

(MIS) began to take hold. Huge budgets were set aside and large corporate organizations were built for data processing. The total audience, however, was still quite small and specialized—those people directly involved with computing technology. In the late 1960s, however, IBM introduced word processing, a concept that became known to a much larger group of people than MIS had been. Organizations such as the International Word Processing Association were born.

Even though word processing focused on the mechanization of typing, primarily a clerical activity, management and other people saw it as a new way to use digital technology in a new place, the office. MIS by contrast, had been confined to a very centralized location.

This development follows Alvin Toffler's concept of the evolution of innovations. A "wave" of innovation begins when traditional ways of thinking about something are unfrozen and new ideas are introduced and adopted. They, in turn, reach a peak, and there is a refreezing as what was once unfamiliar becomes ordinary. Thus, word processing is as commonplace now as typewriters were 20 years ago.

The wave began again in the area of office automation, but with a slightly different slant. In the late 1970s, the first office automation conference was held. Spurred by reports in the press and a lot of advertising, a new application of digital technology—microcomputers—came into public awareness. Though widely known, its use remained relatively specialized until the general population involved itself with the introduction of the personal computer.

I now see the wave of office automation and personal computers dropping off and another wave coming. This next wave has already started with expert systems, knowledge systems, and robotics. Artificial intelligence will begin to take hold. This wave will have a major impact, perhaps even more with blue-collar workers than with white-collar workers. As this wave drops off, I believe we will be left with integrated digital systems to support both industry and the consumer sector.

Besides Toffler's innovation waves there is another way of looking at the evolution of microcomputers, and this is from the perspective of cultural change. As anyone who has tried to get approval for a personal computer in the office can attest, the data processing/management information systems (DP/MIS) organization occupies a powerful sphere of control in the corporate structure. But we can also view this DP/MIS organization more broadly as a sphere of culture. As such it has its own language, and its members share a common awareness that includes experience, materials, and tools. Traditionally, users have been left outside this culture.

These users, who may be financial analysts, lawyers, or executives, make up a very different sphere of overlapping and interacting cultures. Today they are challenging the authority of the DP/MIS culture. By 1983 the mass consumer had acquired 2.5 million personal computers for games, education, and use in personal business. Getting a personal computer was the thing to do.

Perhaps one of the most important aspects of all this personal computer activity was that it involved individuals making decisions about computer acquisitions. As a result there are now about 900,000 personal computers in businesses. All of these are under individual control, except for the 150,000 that were installed through DP/MIS departments.

There is a built-in conflict here, and I think it may prove difficult to integrate these two dissimilar cultures. The corporate side is trying to provide and control tools to get a job done for a justifiable cost, and to offer measurable benefits to the company. Control of PCs offers the multiple benefits of communication, compatibility, service, and economies of scale.

On the other side there is the psychology of the personal computer user: "It's not much, but it's my own." This is a very powerful notion and can provide some real benefits to the corporation. For a marginal cost users are getting what they always wanted— a highly responsive environment. What is needed is to find some way of combining the advantages that come with corporate control and the motivation that comes with individual choice.

I have studied productivity and developed a methodology for productivity measurement, but now I find that no one wants to measure it. The feeling is, "Oh, improved productivity will just come. Let's get some PCs in here." One reason for this response is that we know more about improving individual efficiency than we do about improving corporate productivity. The problem is translating knowledge of the former into the latter. To do this, individuals must reinvest the time saved into some other activity. In other words, corporations don't want shorter workdays, they want individuals to invest the time saved by using personal computers in something that will benefit the corporation. Reinvestment of time is one measure of the productivity that comes from individual use of personal computers.

The acquisition of personal computers raises many issues, both for individuals and corporations. I think the most important ones are architectural. These exist at four different levels in terms of users and the location of data and resources: the individual, the department, the corporation, and the public. The individual needs desktop personal filing, telephone management, and scheduling applications. At the department level, the applications change dramatically and may include accounting tasks and records management.

At the corporate level data processing applications will involve general ledgers, personnel, and inventory. For the public new databases are available through services like videotex and the source, giving access to the Dow Jones industrial average, the *New York Times*, and other information sources.

So many different kinds of data and applications raise many questions. Where do you put the application? If you provide the person who generates a document with word processing, what happens to the document at the departmental level? How do you create some way of moving data to different levels and still keep track of it? Data being transmitted across the corporation poses even more complications. Suppose you are developing an annual report of a new marketing program. It is initially developed by individuals; it is then approved by departments; finally, it is implemented by the corporation. It has to move and be managed. The view of floppy disks as a means of moving and managing information is almost as silly as using punchcards. We need ways to get programs to talk to each other. At present, getting a personal computer to access a corporate database provides nothing more than a glass teletype. Getting information to move between windows is left up to the user and even in machines like the Apple Lisa is very difficult. There are additional problems of communication protocols for moving information.

It becomes apparent that some resolution of these architectural issues is necessary. One of the most important steps we can take is to move away from the notion of the omnipotent and omnipresent IBM personal computer to something that gives much more capability. We need to be heading toward the concept of the per-

sonal workstation environment. The Xerox Star 8010 is a proto-
type of such a concept. Not many people would think of it as a
personal computer. It exists in a network environment, even
though it has up to 25 megabytes of hard disk. With all its short-
comings, it represents the direction in which we are headed: personal computers that don't look or behave like personal computers anymore.

One of the critical things to consider in terms of productivity
and the future of personal computers is what people actually do in
offices. A study of almost 700 people in 7 corporations indicated
that as much as 75 percent of a person's time, especially an executive's time, is spent in communication. The only variable was the
individual style of communicating. Personal computers must
support this function.

Computer messaging is the embodiment of the way terminals
can talk to each other and enable people to send messages back
and forth very rapidly. Electronic mail has been around for a long
time, but we haven't heard anything about how telephony, or
even teleconferencing, is going be integrated into workstation environments. One of the reasons people meet is to share visual information. This can be done from desktop to desktop. Two people
can look at the same data on machines located anywhere in the
world as long as they can be connected through data networks.
Thus, there is no reason they can not interact through an audio
link and a data link to carry on true teleconferencing over long
distances. Intelligent workstations—the personal computers of
the future—will be used to support this kind of communication
network. In diagrammatic form, this network might look like
Figure 1.

All kinds of users—managers, professionals, administrators,
clerical workers, and specialists—are connected in this network,
through a link-up of intelligent workstations, minicomputers, and
maxicomputers. The network forms a gateway to other organizations and ties into other support mechanisms. For example, the
instant a message is sent from this kind of intelligent workstation, it is picked up by support software that automatically
packages it, puts it in an "envelope," interacts with the network,
sends it out, and automatically delivers it if the recipient is logged
on at that moment. In other words, the message can be delivered
instantly.

65

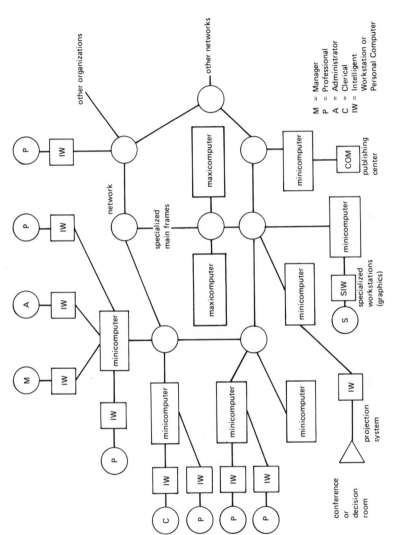

FIGURE 1   Office automation for the organization of the future.

This office of the future is the logical outgrowth of the continuing evolution of computer technology. Today's PCs represent the crest of a wave that has brought popular understanding and public embracing of computer technology. That wave is beginning to recede. It will be replaced by another wave that has already begun to form—the development of integrated digital systems that more fully support the communication and the sharing of information between people.

PART III
MANAGING MICROCOMPUTERS
The Issues

Introduction

*William C. Rosser**

The headline of an advertisement in the September 1983 issue of *Scientific American* asked, "Can a Computer Make You Cry?" The intent of the ad was not frivolous. It was placed by a company that described itself as an association of electronic artists united in a common goal—to fulfill the potential of the personal computer. Its goal is to take the computer beyond its use as a conventional facilitator of unimaginative tasks and use what it calls the wondrous nature of the personal computer to learn more about ourselves. The company sees the personal computer as more than a processor. It can also be a communicator, a communications medium, an interactive tool. It can illustrate our own interest, as human beings, in imagination rather than in predictable procedures, in learning by direct experience rather than by rote or memorization. Finally, the company sees the computer as a transmitter of thoughts and feelings.

Perhaps the question, "Can a Computer Make You Cry?" is not yet very relevant to large organizations. But there are human as well as technological aspects to the personal computer that need attention. After all, personal computers are microcomputers used by individuals. It is this personal side that has particular rele-

*William C. Rosser is vice-president and director of small systems for the Gartner Group, Inc., Stamford, Connecticut.

vance for management. Because of their potential impact on a significant portion of employees, microcomputers may be a uniquely important issue for the large organization and its management.

Considering the rate of growth and popular enthusiasm for personal computers, along with the potentially serious problems they raise, the biggest risk management can take is to wait and do nothing. If the personal computer is an agent for inevitable change, how do we prepare for it? Management has a responsibility to address the potential improvement in the performance of the organization's primary asset—people.

Alastair Omand identifies a whole range of important issues raised by the presence of microcomputers in large organizations. Only a few of these, he says, deserve the attention of top management. The rest are better handled at other organizational levels.

For contributor Roger Sisson, the most important issues are how end-user computing affects the quality of decisions and how microcomputers can be used to facilitate better and more creative decision making in organizations.

Thomas Conrad offers a personal perspective on a set of control-related issues that are especially critical for very large organizations such as the military: procurement, standardization, and centralization.

A Perspective for the Chief Executive Officer

*Alastair I. Omand**

What is so different about the personal computer that it causes management such discomfort? Why is it so hard to figure out which issues deserve top management's attention?

First, the personal computer marketplace is extremely dynamic. Changes in the technology are coming rapidly, apparently too fast for management to know what to buy. Almost daily the trade journals announce new microcomputer products, but nobody knows which are best for the long term. Some of the claims are misleading, and prices are always changing. It is a much different pace from that of the traditional world of large computers.

Second, there is no longer an obvious central point for control. Central management information systems (MIS) departments have traditionally controlled the development and operation of computer systems, as well as the data used by them. End users have worked through programmers or MIS liaison people to get their work done. With personal computers, raw computing power is now available on the desktop of the user, who can do many if not all of the things formerly done by the MIS group.

Further, this computing power is available to the user at rela-

---

*Alastair I. Omand is executive in charge, General Motors Information Systems and Communications Activity, Warren, Michigan.

71

tively low cost. This is significant not only because it signals an economic shift away from the large mainframes, but because many users can now approve the purchase of computers on their own authority. As a result, the marketing tactics of computer vendors have changed. Formerly, they marketed to the MIS people in the organization. Microcomputer vendors now are skirting the MIS department and aiming directly at end users.

Before we can deal with the issues surrounding personal computers, we need to define personal computing and understand where it fits in the overall computing activities of an organization. Personal computing is one of three fundamentally different modes of computing in a corporate environment:

Large-scale computing services represent the traditional mode, in which application systems are managed by MIS professionals rather than by end users. The users provide the data needed, and the MIS organization provides the application programs and processing services to produce the output. Good examples of such applications are payroll processing and product warranty systems. These kinds of applications will continue. The large-scale computing environment typically uses large mainframe computers managed in a restricted facility by the MIS department.

Some organizations in the corporation have adopted an alternative departmental computing mode, often implemented on locally installed minicomputers. Departmental computing is characterized by shared use of computer resources among members of a department. An example would be a production scheduling system for a manufacturing plant.

Then there is the personal computing mode, in which the individual performs tasks unique to the specific job. Personal computing automates the function of the individual, not that of the department, the division, or the corporation.

My definition of personal computing is the use of a computer by an individual to help prepare his or her work product. This definition is important because most microcomputers today are designed for personal computing, that is, for individual users. Thus, the focus is not on payroll processing or shared databases, but on improving the productivity of the individual.

In discussing what the microcomputer management issues really are, we need to draw a clear line between personal computing and departmental computing. Departmental computing systems require a significantly higher level of control since they affect the jobs of many people and may be the repository for corporate records. The danger is that personal computer activities may grow into departmental systems without the necessary controls.

The most frequently discussed issues concerning the use of personal computers in business may be grouped into five categories:

- data management;
- product proliferation;
- acquisition practices;
- level of user maturity;
- the shift in skill sets.

Data management means assuring that the information needs of the corporation are met by the activities that collect data, produce data, or maintain records. This includes providing data access and security. Three specific concerns about data management have been raised relative to the use of personal computers.

The first concern is accessibility of data. The traditional MIS solution to providing data needed by several people was to store it in a central database, in the computers of the central data processing shop. With personal computers, however, data can reside in many places, creating difficulties for access. Knowledge of data location becomes a major problem.

The second concern is consistency and compatibility of data. Without central control of data there is a concern that users will employ different names and formats for the same data. Similarly, they might use the same names for different data, which could lead to a comparison of apples and oranges. To reconcile such diversities could require major conversion efforts and cause delays in responding to business needs.

The third concern is data security. Traditionally, security was ensured by the MIS department with its expertise, elaborate controls, and physically secure facilities. With personal computers responsibility for security is put in the hands of people who may have little or no experience with it. Moreover, with personal computers there is no longer a single logical place to concentrate security expertise and efforts.

A second set of issues relates to the proliferation of personal computer products from many different vendors. This proliferation raises concerns about connectivity. How do we get IBM personal computers to talk to Wang or DEC equipment? How do we get data from one personal computer to another without rekeying?

There are also concerns regarding technical support. How can a large corporation reasonably expect to provide technical support for all of the products used? Must we limit ourselves to only a few vendors? How many vendors will we have to deal with for service or resolution of problems?

Finally, product proliferation raises concerns about duplication of development efforts. Will the same systems have to be developed many times to run on different equipment?

The third set of issues involves acquisition practices. In this area, there is concern that large corporations will miss opportunities for significant cost savings unless a central group coordinates the quantity purchase of personal computers to attain price leverage.

There is also concern about vendor interface. End users are dealing directly with vendors, a responsibility formerly managed by knowledgeable MIS professionals. Users cannot possibly be well informed on all of the available products and their technical complexities. Purchases may not be appropriately justified since many users do not really know why they need a personal computer. In some cases a terminal might do just as well.

Obsolescence is another concern in the area of acquisitions. The rapid advances in microcomputer technology may require new computers to be purchased within a few years. Finally, there is concern about the obligations created by license restrictions where control of software piracy may be difficult or impossible. Will the corporation inadvertently incur legal liabilities?

The fourth set of issues involves the organization's level of experience in using computers. This is illustrated by the "stages of growth" model developed by Dick Nolan. Nolan claims that MIS activities have evolved through a series of stages. The first is initiation, in which computing is first introduced. This is followed by a period of contagion, in which computer applications proliferate throughout the organization in many functional areas. Eventually, the need for controls is recognized. The third stage is thus marked by centralization of many support functions and control procedures in MIS departments. The fourth and later stages are characterized by increased stability and the development of information management disciplines.

The MIS activities of most companies today are in the third stage, marked by central controls. However, the growth of personal computing and end-user experience is generally back in stage one, initiation, or entering stage two, contagion. We are still in the process of learning what personal computing is all about, where the benefits are, and how it is going to work. At the same time developments are spurring rapid increases in use.

This disparity of stages is a source of concern about the growth of personal computing. A major concern in stages one and two, initiation and contagion, lies in the unpredictability of end-user development projects. Without adequate controls in place there are risks that systems will not achieve expected benefits and will not be developed on time and within budget. There are risks that inflexible systems may result. Without proper development techniques for personal computers the systems developed by end users will be difficult to understand, difficult for others to modify, and unresponsive to changing business needs.

In the traditional MIS environment these risks were addressed in the control stage by a variety of systems-development disciplines and review procedures. Well-defined programming guidelines were developed. But no such roadmaps exist to guide users today in developing applications for personal computers.

The last set of issues relates to the shift in skills required by widespread use of personal computers. First, users will become developers, a function formerly in the domain of the MIS community. Yet many users today do not have the skills to manage the development process properly.

Second, end users must learn to manage computers and deal with the risks involved in their use. They will be responsible for backup, data integrity, security, and error detection. In the past the MIS organization has taken care of most of these tasks.

Third, end users must learn to deal with shifting technical trends. You can't install new systems every time a new gimmick hits the market, but you don't want to miss major opportunities because you are locked into obsolete equipment.

The growth in personal computers means a change in the roles of MIS personnel as well. This began with the development of user-friendly languages, information centers, and timesharing and has accelerated with the use of personal computers. Many MIS professionals who have spent their careers as developers will move to user departments; others will become consultants or educators. Both alternatives represent new career paths for MIS people.

All of these issues are important. But which ones should legitimately concern the chief executive officer (CEO) of a company? Where should top management focus its efforts? And who is best suited to deal with the remaining issues?

I believe that some of these issues should not, and in some cases cannot, be addressed through top management control measures. They can be adequately resolved through normal business practices or by further developments in technology. From my perspective, the CEO should focus on the first and last issues outlined above—data management and the shift in skill sets. The other three categories—product proliferation, acquisition practices, and level of user maturity—are best dealt with at lower levels in the organization.

In terms of the first of these lower-level concerns, it is not at all clear that we should try to control product proliferation at this stage. The diversity of products is a good indicator that the potential uses and the best approaches for personal computers are still evolving.

The technology will continue to evolve as well. Although some de facto standards have emerged they may be only temporary. The IBM PC has obviously created some of these standards, but that product represents only one of several plateaus in the evolution of personal computer technology. The next plateau probably belongs to systems running UNIX, the AT&T operating system, and supporting more sophisticated user interfaces derived from the Apple Lisa.

Unfortunately, even though we may be able to identify some of the likely future standards, today's products do not yet support them. The best approach, therefore, is to take advantage of currently available products to meet current needs. The connectivity issue can be addressed where necessary, but setting standards for centralized development and support isn't worth the effort. Centralized developers cannot possibly keep up. Besides, vendors will provide technical support and maintenance to maintain their reputation and survive in the marketplace. The choice of products should be driven primarily by the personal needs of the individuals who are to use them. The current basis of personal computer purchases should be specific needs and opportunities, not anticipated potential.

MIS people can help users sort out alternatives and evaluate the applications. But they should not be given too much authority. Keep the users in charge.

Acquisition practices for computers are important, as they are for any expenditure. But the primary responsibility in this area rests with an organization's purchasing staff. They should be looking for equivalent products at lower prices and they should recognize and pursue opportunities for volume discounts. In fact, this is much easier to do for microcomputers than it ever was for data processing equipment. There are many interchangeable products, particularly peripherals like printers and display monitors. Purchasing people also have the responsibility for seeing that license agreements are reasonable. They should be allowed to do their jobs.

Similarly, the investment decision should be controlled by traditional financial procedures. Budgets and appropriation procedures are no less applicable to personal computers than to any other equipment bought to run a business.

For the most part major investments are not involved. Thus, the risks are minimal. Most personal computers purchased now should have paid for themselves by the time they are clearly obsolete. Savings opportunities shouldn't be missed because it might be possible to make a better decision later. There will continue to be uncertainties.

The disparity in the level of user experience between MIS departments and users of personal computers is undeniable. While MIS organizations are busy controlling their resources and tuning their operations, the whole microcomputer marketplace is in the contagion stage. This needn't cause great concern. It should be exploited, not controlled.

When data processing activities were in the contagion stage million-dollar investments in equipment and development projects were involved. The risks were high that projects would not meet expectations on time, within budget. This is not the case with personal computers. With small-scope systems the investment is small. The business impact is focused on the job of a single individual. The development investment may be simply one individual's learning curve, not the expenditure of years of effort by full-time technical experts.

Finally, auditors should be allowed to do their job. Their responsibility is to assure that good business practices are followed. If there is concern that such practices might be ignored with the use of personal computers, auditors should be called in.

When many of the personal computer issues are handled at appropriate, lower organizational levels, the CEO can focus attention on the more critical issues.

Data management is one of the most complex of these critical concerns. To understand how the growth of personal computers affects data management it is helpful to identify the functions:

• Business processes, particularly those that involve multiple departments, should be streamlined through business systems analysis.

• Interdepartmental interfaces must be clearly defined and supported with communications facilities to assure data availability.

• Sources of business data must be defined to assure that the proper controls are exercised and necessary records are kept.

• Data security must be assured through the identification of risks and the definition of control requirements and precautions.

These functions focus primarily on mainstream business systems rather than on personal computing. They involve multiple departments rather than the individual. But there is little doubt that personal computers, like their users, will become participants in these larger systems. Personal computers will be used to process corporate data; they will thus influence the development of larger systems that go beyond the scope of personal computing.

The CEO can take three steps to ensure that data management is properly addressed in the area of personal computing as well as in other areas of the organization.

The first step is to place organizational responsibility for data management. Data management is a coordination and control function. It requires the participation of all departments, but it also requires a focal point of responsibility. General Motors is encouraging both divisions and corporate staffs to create a department called Business Information Management. Its activities include the MIS functions, but with a new mission. Rather than controlling the use of computer technology, its function is to help other departments exploit the technology while providing the coordination and control necessary for data management.

The next step for the CEO is to initiate the definition of appropriate policies and practices, mainly in the area of data security and integrity. The data management organization should lead this effort, but it requires the participation of other parts of the organization as well. These measures must address the new risks associated with personal computers. Personal computers are located in offices instead of data centers, and they store large amounts of data on diskettes that are easy to transport. These and related factors create new security risks that must be faced.

Finally, the CEO should initiate policies and practices that control the scope of personal computing. Such policies should be reinforced by data management efforts. It is fairly easy for a personal computing effort to grow into a departmental system. A red flag must go up when an individual starts maintaining departmental records on a personal computer. Although various individuals need copies of corporate data, the organization must not depend on them and their personal computers as the sole source of such data.

The second critical area for CEO concern involves personnel. The growth of personal computing is just one aspect of the increasing involvement of end users in the application of computers. As a result, the responsibilities and many of the skills required for computer application development must migrate from the MIS organization to the end user.

For this migration to be effective the CEO must be prepared to make a significant investment in education. This will take the form of classes, seminars, and the cost of a learning curve for users, all of which translates into dollars.

End users must be trained to manage the new responsibilities that come with personal computing. First they must gain an adequate understanding of the general concepts of computer and telecommunications technology. Then they must learn about microcomputers in particular. They must be skilled in proper techniques for systems design and security.

MIS professionals will also require education. Some will be relocated in user departments and will need a greater understanding of the user's business. Many others will refocus their careers from systems developers to consultants for end users and must develop consulting skills.

The education effort will also need to extend beyond users of computers. People in purchasing departments must have an increased understanding of technology in general and will need to develop selection criteria for various vendor products. This will require a much greater knowledge of personal computers than they have today. Auditors must have a greater awareness of the latest microcomputer technology as well. They will need to be aware of the risks involved in using these machines and be able to assess alternative measures.

All of these educational needs will cost money, and management should expect to spend it to get the most benefit from the new technologies. Our work force must get smart on the risks and the opportunities if the investment in personal computers is to yield the desired return.

In short, here is my advice to organizations trying to cope with the personal computer invasion. Don't try to stop it. Don't try to standardize the technology. Don't limit the user's innovation and initiative. Instead, focus your attention on the critical success factors. Manage your data resources to assure that the right people continue to have access to the right data. Educate users so they can take advantage of the technology, properly manage it, and deal with the attendant risks.

Dissertations have been written about the disparity of investment in productivity between production workers and knowledge workers. Personal computing is one of the most promising opportunities to increase knowledge-worker productivity. It is management's responsibility to make sure that people have every chance to exploit it.

Managing Microcomputers and End-User Computing
Some Critical Issues

*Roger L. Sisson**

Much of U.S. industry needs help. Proper use of data and computer power might provide part of the needed assistance. An example of the kind of help I'm referring to comes from the steel industry, one of those most in need. With access to a computer and the right data, a cost analyst at one company we worked with provided significant information about his company's product profits.

This analyst had spent part of his career in the sales department. Soon after he was assigned to cost analysis duties, he was given access to a terminal, a powerful fourth-generation language system, and data—particularly invoice and cost data.

Until this point no one had been able to explain variations in company profits. As a result of his work in sales, however, the analyst knew that costs and profits were reported only on a product line basis, and that one line accounted for 60 percent of the company's business. With his computer-aided tools he was able, in a few days, to analyze the profitability of individual products in the major line. This had many benefits: it explained the month-to-month variation in profits; it pinpointed areas where cost reductions would pay off; and it provided guidance to sales. This analy-

---

*Roger L. Sisson is president of Sisson, Michaelis Associates, Inc., Swarthmore, Pennsylvania, and lecturer at the Wharton School of Business.

sis will not turn the entire steel industry from loss to profit, but it is helping one company come closer to profitability.

Such analysis is becoming routine, an example of the payoff use of computers by nonspecialists. But this use of computers by non-data processing professionals in large organizations raises some important issues.

Two issues are critical: the quality of decisions that result when decision analysis is facilitated by microcomputers or other computer-based aids, and the security of data and programs from theft or manipulation for unauthorized purposes. There are also less critical, but still important, administrative issues.

Before looking at these issues we need to understand what we mean when we talk about this exploding phenomenon of end-user computing. Computing in this context means accessing and performing analyses on data to support decision making. The data usually come from existing files but may be entered by the analyst. Computing also covers the case in which the user is installing a small, local, complete system that includes entering and updating data and producing standard reports as well as analytic outputs.

The end user is a non-data processing professional who is performing the sort of computing just described. In other words, the main mission of the end user is some function other than data processing. He or she may be performing market research, financial analysis, contract administration, or budget preparation.

In considering end users and their use of computers in relationship to the organization, we may for the moment ignore the difference between terminals and microcomputers as the end user's tool. Whatever the tool, the principal issue is: *Does the availability of computer power facilitate better decisions?*

Over the last 30 years the data processing profession has developed important standards, guidelines, and procedures designed to facilitate the use of the computer, to make program maintenance easier and less expensive, and to insure the integrity and security of data. Do the hundreds of thousands of new end users have to come up with their own sets of standards and procedures through long and sometimes bitter experience? Or can data processing professionals help end users? These questions suggest a third important end-user computing issue that, along with quality of decisions and security, deserves attention. This is the issue of administration of information processes and resources. Let us look at each of these issues in some detail.

As background to a discussion of the effect of end-user computing on decision quality, I would like to introduce the notion of *distributed creativity*. This is my name for the much discussed concept that organizational success depends on innovation and a striving for excellence at *all levels* of the organization.

In the book *In Search of Excellence* (Harper and Row, New York: 1982) Peters and Waterman remark that in the excellent firms, "quality and service were invariable hallmarks. To get them, of course, everyone's cooperation is required, not just mighty labors from the top 200" (p. 24). Elsewhere in the book, they offer an example: "3M has been described as 'so intent on innovation that its essential atmosphere seems not like that of a large corporation but rather a loose network of laboratories and cubbyholes populated by feverish inventors and dauntless entrepreneurs who let their imaginations fly in all directions'.... They encourage private risk taking, and support good tries" (p. 15).

In more philosophical terms, one goal of a large organization is to strike a balance between authority and anarchy. Somewhere between these two extremes lies a freedom to create modified by controls to insure that the organization is cohesive and has direction. The best means of accomplishing this is the major management theory question of this decade.

One way of answering the question goes like this: Wisdom comes from experience and usually correlates with level in the organization. We assume the chief executive officer is wise. Therefore, important decisions should be made at the top. We should centralize the decision making and the analytic support.

Actual experience, however, has shown that the "top" is too far from the action. There one loses touch with customers, vendors, operation, shops, and labs. To restate Peters and Waterman, the best process is to transmit the wisdom through the culture and to place most of the decision making where the action is. If the culture transmits wise values and constraints, decisions made at lower levels will be based on the best information in a context that guides the decisions with experience and wisdom of top management. End-user computing can help both to provide information and to transmit some aspects of the cultural wisdom. How does it do this?

Creative leaps of imagination are not inductive. They do not derive logically from the data. But creativity does not occur in an environment devoid of data either. The process of studying data seems to facilitate innovative thinking. Since the end user often cannot predict which data are relevant, access is needed to a variety of files with data about the environment, the history and current status of operations, policies and rules, and resource availability. The end user may be performing any of a number of management analysis tasks: looking for exceptions, for opportunities, for measures of current status and progress, for alternatives, or for estimates of the consequences of adopting an alternative. An innovative insight may come at any point during any of these studies.

There are of course costs and risks in providing computer resources to many end users. Is the cost worth the benefits from improved decisions? I think the benefits significantly outweigh the risks and costs. This judgment is based on two beliefs: first, that distributed creativity is valuable and is facilitated by end-user computing, and second, that our culture is particularly able to be creative if given the right tools.

Especially in the United States, we learn from childhood to do things ourselves. At great national expense we prefer automobiles to mass transit so that we can go where we want when we want. We have even learned how to drive trucks to move our belongings ourselves rather than use a trucking service. The ultimate demonstration of distributed creativity in our culture is the prevalence of entrepreneurs and the proliferation of small enterprises.

With this cultural heritage it is not surprising that managers and analysts want to handle their own decision support and the computing that goes with it. The rise of personal computing was predictable given our culture of individual initiative, even if most data processing professionals, blinded by their own expertise, did not forecast it.

But a desire to do things on one's own is not enough. You can't rent a drive-it-yourself truck if the only trucks available are 18-wheelers requiring special training and hard work to drive. And you won't rent a truck if the closest rental office is several hundred miles away.

Until a couple of years ago computers were like 18-wheelers—

they were inaccessible. Communication facilities were not extensive; terminals were slow and awkward. Operating systems were unfriendly, making it nearly impossible, even for professionals, to get into the system. And if you did it cost an arm and a leg.

Six things have occurred recently to make end-user computing a reality, to make it easy for the user to rent (connect to) the systems, to drive, to read the maps (use software), and to pay for the gas (the computer resources):

• Inexpensive on-line computer resources became available through efficient mainframes and reasonably easy-to-use video terminals or through microcomputers.

• Operating systems are now user-friendly.

• Fourth- and fifth-generation language systems are now available, allowing end users to communicate with computer systems without knowing programming languages.

• A large number of people are either knowledgeable about computers or at least not afraid of them.

• Decisionmakers have a desire, and usually a real need, to process information rather than fly by the seat of their pants.

• End users recognize that the data they need is available somewhere in the organization's computer files.

These breakthroughs mean we can now "do it ourselves." End-user computing is here. With 8.3 million terminals and 2.4 million micros in the United States, the 300,000 data processing professionals are outnumbered by end users 33 to 1.

Now that we have the tools, will their use result in better decisions? Although I have seen no formal studies on changes in the quality of decisions when extensive computer facilities are available to the decisionmaker, there is some evidence. A survey now in progress of end-user support groups (information centers) suggests that end-user computing does make contributions to the bottom line. Alloway and Quillard (*MIS Quarterly* 7(2):1983, 27–41) also found, as a result of a survey, that managers certainly want decision-support computer facilities.

According to Peters and Waterman, Abernathy, Clark, and Kantrow (*Industrial Renaissance.* Basic Books, New York: 1983, p. 21), and other management researchers, encouraging innovation at all levels is vital to an organization's continued success. If this is so, the availability of data-analyzing capabilities and good end-user computing support should in many cases improve the decision-making process.

There is also a flip side to using computers in decision making. A computer, whether a micro or a mainframe, is a very powerful tool. As with any powerful tool it is possible to use it to make powerful mistakes, inadvertently or fraudulently. One of the potentially dangerous mistakes is a bad decision, because it may have far-reaching consequences. Therefore, it is important to know how decisions are being made by end users, to know that they are being made in reasonable ways and with the organization's objectives in mind. This concern was illustrated by an official of the Bank of America who said to me, "We wonder how all those loan officers are deciding on loans with their IBM PCs and Visicalcs."

The freedom of the individual to innovate, given the right tools, is unique in the West and most prevalent in the United States. Thus, I believe that the cost of *not* providing modern information tools to end users is much greater than the cost of a few bad decisions made more easily by the use of these powerful tools. Our successful organizations have always depended on their employees to improve them, to innovate, and to advance their welfare. One characteristic of these organizations is that they provide nearly everyone with the tools needed to be creative. A period of increasing international competition is not the time to hold back.

Once we agree that good end-user computing resources do lead to better decisions, we can go on to consider the difference between end-user support from terminal-based mainframes and from microcomputers. (Mainframe here means any large computer or minicomputer controlled by a data processing staff.) The mainframe/micro choice must be viewed from the benefits side. Which will do more to improve the quality of decision making? I think the choice today depends on the specific system. There are three determining factors:

• Access to relevant data may be difficult on a stand-alone micro, but if good communications are available the micro is no different from a terminal.

• A mainframe system with very good response time and an array of effective, user-friendly software might provide better support of decision making than a micro. But many mainframe timesharing systems do not meet those objectives. They are slow, and good software for end users does not exist or is not made available. In these cases the end user will find the micro preferable.

• Mainframes are expensive because of the multiuser overhead and the communications costs.

If we recognize that any micro can act as a terminal and do much more, and that micros are not much more expensive than a terminal, microcomputers will probably be the preferred solution in terms of benefits.

Three additional developments will clinch the micro's advantage over terminals: the capacity of micros is increasing; the friendliness of micro software is improving; and the facilities to transfer data between micro and mainframe, preferably in a way transparent to the user, are becoming available.

Soon the micro, combined with communications to the sources of data in the mainframe, will be the dominant solution. (This combination of microprocessor and communication, accompanied by good software, is termed by some a "workstation.")

In addition to these policy and technical considerations, we cannot forget the individuality factor in our culture and how it will affect the use of micros. Taking away or refusing to allow someone to have a micro will be like taking away or refusing someone the use of an automobile. That is unthinkable in a country where we have a hard time preventing even drunks from using automobiles.

End-user computing, largely supported by micros, is obviously valuable. If there is some reason to slow down or suppress the use of micros it must be because of other issues, such as security or administrative decisions.

Security is a critical issue: making a system secure may also limit its flexibility and usefulness. Such limitations prevent or slow down the distribution of capabilities that aid creativity. Therefore, the goal is to make the security procedures easy to use yet relatively impenetrable. A single key is not hard to use. A lock requiring two people and two keys gets to be a nuisance.

When I was designing systems I had little concern for safety. The auditors were there to worry about that, and their specific suggestions would be implemented. Security, however, was not allowed to get in the way of ease of operation. Today I think greater concern is warranted. When thousands of people are accessing sensitive corporate or agency data, the probability is that someone will remove competitively sensitive data on a floppy disk. A floppy disk is convenient; it is easy to transfer data to it; it can hold hundreds of pages of data. A person can walk out of a building with it unobserved. The contents need not be identifiable externally. How does a security guard know what is on one?

There is also the well-publicized problem of illegal access by telephone. Since solutions to this kind of unauthorized access are known, the problem falls into the administrative area. It should be possible to detect and trap unauthorized dial-in access.

Access to a computer system is possible not only directly through the normal log-on process, but also by tapping communications links and by removal of media such as floppy disks. To eliminate loss through these means some form of encryption is required to protect the data even when the media are compromised, or to make decoding so expensive that potential thieves are dissuaded.

These measures are expensive, as are any security measures. To justify them the potential loss from a security breach must be greater than the cost of the security measures. The organizations we have worked with limit their security measures to password systems. Some depend only on the log-on password; others have protection at the file level, so the end user must know two or three passwords. A few have additional password protection at the operating systems level. I know of no commercial firm that uses encryption in relation to the kind of end-user computing we are discussing. Ultimately, most organizations depend on a trustworthy work force.

Microcomputers are removed from the direct control of the mainframe, and therefore are not guided by data processing standards. Does the use of micros create additional security problems? To answer this we must distinguish between external and internal breaches of security. In terms of external attempts to invade the system, it seems to me that micros do not add problems. Physically locking the micro and any removable media may be necessary in some cases. However, data down-loaded to a micro is not at greater risk than data printed out, or data put on a floppy disk, or microfiche, or any other removable media. In relation to internal security leaks, the micro, as a powerful information processor, may provide opportunities for access and removal not previously available. Internal security is ultimately still a matter of auditing and personnel policies, not technology.

The final set of issues are those that, I believe, can be resolved in most organizations by normal administrative procedures and proper computer-user interfacing. These issues are the effects of bad data, data integrity, the problem of transferring end-user-developed programs, and the question of who pays for added computer capacity, the wasting of resources, and the proliferation of languages.

Poor Data. Are decisions supported by computer-based analysis deficient because of poor data? This may be an important question where data from outside sources are used. The quality of outside data must be checked just as the quality of received parts or materials is checked. (In a few places it may be advisable to check the quality of the internal data as well.) Data quality really involves two questions. Is the decisionmaker better off with no data or with data that may have some errors? If flawed data are used will the power of the computer-based analytic tools in some way amplify the errors?

There are several responses to this problem. Obviously, care should be taken to prevent bad data whether micros, terminals, or adding machines are being used. In each case the end user is more likely to know the data and therefore be better able to catch errors than corporate staff or others. In fact, the power of the computer may help the end user find errors by performing various consistency and trend analyses. Thus, end user access to data may have an additional benefit of making the data more accurate. Further, the kind of decision-support analysis we are discussing may be insensitive to occasional data errors. Of course, management should always be aware that recommendations and analytic results may be based on poor data. End-user computing should not aggravate this situation if administrative procedures are followed to keep the data as clean as possible and to remind the staff to check the data and the reasonableness of the results.

Data integrity. Can the end user affect the operational data in corporate files? If so, can the integrity of the data be assured? Can the changes made by an end user be audited?

The only way to insure the integrity of data is to maintain all the controls that data processing has painfully learned: good editing, effective audit logs and procedures, and good recovery processes. There is no reason to relax these for the benefit of end users. The only way master files should be updated is by the normal, well-controlled transaction processing system.

Transfer of data and programs. What about files that a user maintains independent of the mainframe systems? Should the data and programs developed by an end user be considered private, scratch pad material or should some mechanism be installed to allow sharing of this material? If the end user is working on a mainframe the data and programs are at least accessible, even if they are not properly structured and documented. But data and programs developed on a micro may be as inaccessible as those on paper. Some organizations are in fact taking the attitude that the data and programs developed by an end user on a micro are the same as material on paper. If the user leaves, the new occupant must develop his or her own routine and data. Peers who need to do similar processing must develop their own tools, perhaps with the informal help of the first end user. The results of the end user's analyses are submitted in reports (with appropriate appendixes) in the usual way. The data and routines not included in the appendixes are no longer of interest; they are throw-away materials.

If the organization decides that it does want to capture programs or data that are on a micro and judged to be valuable, administrative procedures must be instituted just as they are for data processing professionals. These will not be easy to enforce, however, because there are many decentralized end users who have little interest in data processing's problems. The only other alternative is to prohibit the development of "systems" on micros and allow such development only in a mainframe context.

Resource use and charge-back. If we provide many end users with the opportunity to use computers, and especially if we make it easy for them with effective languages and other software, the demand for computer capacity will soar. The issue is whether additional capacity is a good investment. If end users are helping to make decisions that significantly increase the effectiveness of the organization, the service it provides, or its profits, the cost of the computer resources may be well justified.

But only management can justify this resource use. To do this, it should know what the end user is doing and how that work contributes to the organization. The data processing people, who normally have to justify the increase in capacity, do not know the benefits side of the justification. Therefore, charge-back of all computer costs is mandatory, and every company we have worked with or surveyed that supports end-user computing has a charge-back of real budget dollars. The budget transfer from charge-back is prima facie evidence for the data processing department that the computer use has value; the customer paid for it. If those in top management do not agree, they have to discuss it with the end users.

Wasted resources. If people are given relatively free access to computers will they waste the resources? Waste can occur in several ways:

• trying to solve problems by random trial and error (with or without models);
• computing rather than thinking, researching, or getting out and talking with customers, employees, and other individuals;
• using poorly written, inefficient routines;
• trying to write programs instead of using packaged software or higher-level languages.

Unlike scrap in a metals production process, the scrap in an information process is invisible. It is not easy to identify waste, so it may become prevalent and expensive.

People waste information tools all the time. Who keeps track of pencil and paper wastage? Is a few minutes of computer time spent on an inefficient routine worse than throwing away some sheets of paper from a bad draft? To answer, one has to look at cost and benefit. For example, a little waste in a process that costs a couple hundred dollars but may be saving 10 times that in reduced costs or improved sales is not worth concern.

Choice of languages. Effective end-user computing that leads to better decisions requires languages that end users can handle. A major issue is the selection of the proper languages and supporting software systems. This is a technical topic, but it should not be overlooked as a management issue. It is important also to standardize languages throughout the organization to prevent a Tower of Babel. Every group we have contacted has settled on a few basic language tools: for reporting, for statistical analysis, for financial planning, for electronic mail, and sometimes for word processing. (In all cases there was one set of standard software for the mainframe and one set for micros.)

If my thesis about distributed creativity is correct, end-user computing, with micros where justified, is appropriate. Through a good end-user support group, sometimes called an information center, local managers can receive information support of all types, not only with hardware but with software and training. However, some controls should be attached to these support efforts:

• Use passwords properly. Change them frequently. Tie them to people and terminals, not groups.

• Control the use of floppy disks and prevent unauthorized removal of data.

• Isolate the user from the operating system with a friendly menu and command-driven front end.

• Don't let end users update main files except through batch processes with good edits and controls or through on-line systems with formal edit, audit, and recovery procedures.

• Decide between a throw-away or a share policy for user-developed, decision-aiding programs. If sharing is chosen, build the infrastructure to support it.

• Provide good user training. Users tend to follow the instructions given, and good training can help reduce waste, correct inefficient routines, and promote data security and integrity.

• Use a real money charge-back system and let the end users' manager worry about waste. Allocate disk space carefully—it is relatively expensive. Limiting disk space constrains the extent of data and thus indirectly controls how large and complex the user's systems can be.

Distributed creativity is an important national asset. It can help the revitalization of industry and the recovery of the U.S. position in international competition. End-user computing, supported by micros or terminals and by a good support staff, promotes distributed creativity. Microcomputers in particular can encourage innovation and good decision making at all levels of the organization. No longer just an executive gadget or a local data processor, micros have become, I believe, an important link in rebuilding our national strength.

Regaining Control Through Centralized Action

Thomas D. Conrad*

The issues involved in managing microcomputers can be summed up in a few words: to standardize or not, to facilitate or not, to control or not, to wait or not. We face aspects of these issues daily in the Air Force.

Standardization presents a special problem to the military because of rotation policies. As user-operators move from one assignment to another, they are exposed to different systems, equipment, and database management systems (DBMSs). As a result, we have continual training and logistics problems. How do we resupply a microcomputer in Egypt, Grenada, Korea, the Philippines, or Okinawa? How do we handle backward compatibility? How do we handle the portability of data as we move around the world? How do we handle the portability of the hardware itself?

Procurement raises another set of issues. Should it be centralized or decentralized? Do we purchase computers with capital funds or with operational funds? This is not an insignificant problem in the military services. Do we buy or lease? This issue is being debated in Congress. Do we use a lowest-cost acquisitions policy or do we consider technical merit along with cost? For years the military services have been prodded into awarding con-

*Thomas D. Conrad is former deputy assistant secretary, information systems management, Office of the Assistant Secretary of the Air Force.

tracts to the lowest bidder. Are hardware and software acquisitions single or separate procurements?

How should the whole proposal and contract award process work? Should a request for a proposal (RFP) be on a requirement basis, in effect designing the computer, or should specifications be strictly functional? Should the development of specifications and the evaluation of proposals be centralized or decentralized? How should we handle multiple awards? Do we choose in-house or contract maintenance?

All of these issues grew out of some initial observations I made when I first came to Washington. I realized there was a proliferation of all kinds of microcomputers in the Air Force. In fact, many were not really business computers at all; they were more like home computers, but they were being used in critical areas of our national defense. Sometimes they were purchased with capital funds, sometimes with operational funds, sometimes with slush funds, and sometimes with private funds. Personal computers, owned by individuals, were being used operationally. When those individuals rotated out, they took their computers with them. Such practices did not seem very wise from a business viewpoint, particularly when that business was national defense.

My first step was to place a moratorium on the purchase of microcomputers. For almost a year no approval was given to purchase any microcomputers. Besides catching everyone's attention, this step stimulated cooperation in the expeditious development of specifications and a procurement strategy.

My next action was to convene an advisory council. The group of about 33 appointees met in November 1982. It was not the usual committee, because I had decision-making power. Thus, council members who had the most influential or convincing arguments would actually determine the direction we would take.

We began by developing a requirements contract for microcomputers. No minimum or maximum quantities were specified. Nor did the contract require that any money be available for purchases. Instead, it simply said that if any micros at all were purchased over the period of the one-year contract (with two one-year options for renewal on the part of the Air Force) they would be purchased under the terms of the contract, from whomever won the award. (In fact, when we placed the RFP on the street and even when we awarded the contract we had no assurance that we would buy any computers, because we had no money whatsoever behind the contract.)

Further, the contract set only minimum specifications—for example, the size of the disk and the size of the screen—and therefore was not a functional RFP. It was coordinated with and approved through the General Services Administration (GSA) and became a joint acquisition of the Air Force, Navy, and Marine Corps.

We received requests for the RFP from 330 different companies or organizations. About two weeks after the release of the RFP we held the preproposal vendor conference, which was attended by 155 people. We received 32 proposals, a record for the Air Force Computer Acquisition Center. Of those 32 proposals, we eliminated 17 that were deemed unsuitable.

I had stated publicly that it was not the Air Force's intent to award the contract solely on the basis of the lowest bid. Instead, the award was to be based on three integrated considerations: cost, technical excellence, and postsale contractor support. The RFP stated that cost would carry a weight of 40 to 60 percent. The exact weight was not made public and, in fact, was not even determined until after we had initially evaluated the proposals. Technical excellence would have a weight of 30 to 50 percent, and contractor support counted for 10 to 20 percent.

The final award would be determined by an objective, detailed scoring of points weighted for technical excellence, based on an established range set up in a scoring model. Excellence points were given for those items offered that were above and beyond the minimum specifications. For example, we specified a 5-megabyte hard disk as an optional item. Those vendors who offered a larger capacity hard disk earned excellence points. We also gave excellence points for a separate keyboard, for the capacity of floppy disks, for different database systems, and for certain spreadsheets. It was possible for a vendor to get as many as 1,000 extra points for technical excellence.

To select a tentative winning proposal, we integrated a value of low cost, technical excellence points, and contractor support. The integration exercise was interesting because we had never before brought together cost and technical excellence points. One possible way to do this was to take the vendor's bid and divide by the total technical excellence points given. We could then put a value on these points, and whoever had the lowest cost per point would receive the work.

The fallacy of this method was that it gave no consideration to the vendor who had no technical excellence points. What was the cost of his points if he had none? Such a bidder obviously had an acceptable system because he had survived the competition, but with zero points for technical excellence he could not win the award. To solve this problem we established a base value for the basic offering. Every system that met the minimum requirement was worth $18 million. We subtracted $18 million from every bid, divided the remainder by the technical excellence points, arrived at a value per point, and integrated that value with the cost.

Best and final offers brought prices down substantially, and a tentative winner was selected. Following the selection, a live test demonstration resulted in a rescoring and reduction of points that caused us to reevaluate and go to the next apparent winner. That vendor came out of the live test with more technical excellence points than he had originally.

In October 1983 we awarded the contract to Zenith Data Systems for their Z100 base systems at a cost substantially below what was available in the market or through GSA (probably close to a 55 percent discount on the retail price). In my estimation this "exercise" saved the Air Force and therefore taxpayers some $36 million. As its originator, I am quite pleased with this centralized action and its result.

PART IV
MANAGING MICROCOMPUTERS
Case Studies

Introduction

*Rhoda W. Canter**

If grappling with microcomputer technology trends, their implications, and the management issues involved is difficult on a theoretical level, developing and implementing strategies uniquely adapted to individual organizations is an even more awesome task. For every theoretical issue there are multiple practical questions to answer:

- How much control is needed over microcomputers, where and when is it needed, and through what means can it be applied most effectively?
- Should microcomputers be interconnected or connected with minicomputers and mainframes? What is the most systematic approach to defining appropriate uses of the different technologies? What are the implications for the organizational structure and skills of the information processing community?
- How can the most effective microcomputer applications be identified and what are the implications for the functional management community?
- What pace of implementation will best suit the needs, desires, and capabilities of potential users of microcomputer?
- Should management responsibilities for information processing be reassigned and, if so, how?

*Rhoda W. Canter is a principal of Arthur Young and Company, Washington, D.C.

• How can an organization establish education and training goals for introducing new technologies? What programs will ensure that these goals are achieved effectively?

• How should concerns about data administration be addressed? What are the organization's information resources? Where are these resources? Who is responsible for them? How can security of information resources be achieved?

• How can microcomputer components be acquired, maintained, and operated most effectively?

The list only scratches the surface.

Difficult as these challenges are, managers in large organizations must come to grips with them. The five case studies that follow present a variety of large organizations and their efforts to manage emerging microcomputer technologies. The organizations represent several major segments of industry—manufacturing, insurance and financial institutions, state government, and the military services. They also represent a broad spectrum of management styles, ranging from overt central control to control through persuasion to a laissez-faire approach. In each case senior management has addressed universal issues and made particular decisions with respect to successful management in a given environment.

The balance and movement between management and practice in the realm of technology is intricate. Through these five case studies of successes, failures, and lessons learned we catch glimpses of a common process. The process encompasses analysis of the organization's culture; setting strategic goals in concert with that culture; planning, organizing, and controlling to meet strategic goals; and marketing the organization's approach to the entire work force. This process, distilled from the maze of particulars, can contribute significantly to management theory and, in turn, to management practice in large organizations everywhere.

Productivity Through Automation

John J. Alexander, Jr. *

Automation is widely viewed as a key way to increase productivity. At Reynolds Metals Company the use of automation to improve productivity is the focus of the company's planning and development efforts for the 1980s. Its specific objective is to use automation to double the productivity of its salaried work force by 1990. A brief profile of the company will give some idea of the extent of this effort.

Reynolds is a Fortune 100 producer of primary and recycled aluminum. Operations are conducted by 12 divisions that explore, mine, ship, and refine bauxite; reduce alumina to primary aluminum; recycle scrap aluminum; and fabricate aluminum into a wide range of products. An international division manufactures and sells overseas. About one-third of our 30,000 employees are salaried and work in 50 plants, 25 sales offices, and the corporate headquarters in Richmond, Virginia.

Management, of course, is the key word in such an effort. And just like the management of any other corporate function, managing information processing is itself a process. Specific tasks required to carry out the process can be identified. In addition to the conventional maxim "plan, organize, and control," I would add "strategize, rationalize, and market."

*John J. Alexander, Jr. is senior vice-president of management information systems, MCI Telecommunications Corporation, Washington, D.C.; and former corporate director of administration, Reynolds Metals Company.

Reynolds' planning process for automation was developed during 1978 and 1979. The planning cycle begins in the spring when an update and an automation planning manual is issued, telling all division and plant automation managers what they need to do to develop an automation plan for their unit. Corporate management provides some structure and asks managers to detail their plans and programs.

The deadline for responses is October and coincides with the completion of the company's annual business planning cycle. Reynolds encourages but does not require interaction between business and automation planning. The analysis of the results of one cycle consumes the October-to-May period and provides input and structure for the next cycle. Thus, planning is a continuous process. The first five planning cycles are summarized below.

• *1979–80 planning cycle.* In this first planning cycle hardware was standardized and data was identified as an issue. A study was commissioned that provided an understanding of logical and physical views of data and the tools for analysis.

• *1980–81 planning cycle.* The corporate staff proposed a network, which has been installed, and the salaried employee was identified as a target for major productivity improvement.

• *1981–82 planning cycle.* The System/38 was added to the approved hardware list, experimentation with personal computers was encouraged, and IBM's business systems planning (BSP) technology was introduced.

• *1982–83 planning cycle.* The IBM Displaywriter and personal computer were added to the approved hardware line, and a study of information architecture was begun.

• *1983–84 planning cycle.* The need for additional central computer capacity to keep balance with the growth of distributed processing was determined.

From the early planning cycles we concluded that although the annual planning process is essential, looking at information requirements for the short term is not sufficient. We had to take a much longer look, and that required a strategic goal. In 1980 we articulated such a longer-term planning goal.

This goal was to provide all salaried employees with the automation tools they need to manage the information necessary to perform their jobs and double their productivity by 1990. In defining this goal we also described the rationale behind it, projected the rate at which it could be achieved, identified the major roadblocks to accomplishing it, developed a marketing approach to delivering the necessary automation tools, and limned the kind of changes in the organizational culture that would have to occur to achieve the goal.

Although this is a very ambitious goal, the company believes it must be accomplished if Reynolds is to be productive and profitable over the next decade. Seeking a rationale, we looked at what our salaried employees do and recognized that information plays a very large role in their jobs. They receive information in the form of memos or reports and store some of it, mostly in five-drawer file cabinets. They use salaried secretaries to retrieve it or go after it themselves, look at it, manipulate it, reformat it, analyze it, and send it on to somebody else. Automation can provide some support for every one of these information processing operations. It is not going to reduce the human factor to zero, but it can increase productivity.

Based on our projections about rates of change in cost of automation components and people, we projected that 20 percent per year reduction in the cost of automation components is sustainable for this decade. In the past five years, people have increased in cost an average of 10 percent per year at Reynolds.

In some areas we have carefully tracked what a work group was doing before automation was applied and what was required to accomplish the same tasks after automation was applied. In these cases we can demonstrate improvements in productivity ranging from 100 to over 500 percent.

The major roadblock to automation lies in taking the conventional approach to developing automation solutions to business problems. This approach calls for custom-designed systems to solve the information requirements of an individual or a group of individuals. At Reynolds what we call a system typically takes about three years to develop and directly affects about 15 people. With a limited set of resources, 150 people at Reynolds build and maintain systems. Half maintain the old systems and half build new systems.

Using the 1980 work force as a base we assumed that the 1,000 individuals then using automation were representative of the total. Extrapolating the systems work done from 1977 through 1979 to the entire work force yielded a backlog of approximately three decades needed to automate all 11,000 salaried employees. We concluded that we needed a new approach.

The alternative we developed is a marketing approach to providing information services within a major corporation. Marketing provides the answers to three critical questions: Who is our customer? What is our product? How is the product distributed?

We began by recognizing that our "customer" is the individual employee who uses a computer or terminal. We classified these individuals by need and identified common information-handling requirements. This allowed us to organize the market of employees into a handful of segments and to develop delivery vehicles for automation services to reach each segment.

When analyzing such a market, it is helpful to consider whether it consists of all employees; various segments of employees like managers, professionals, clerks and secretaries, and other individuals defined as office workers; or all salaried employees. Reynolds settled on the last category as the most appropriate for its automation program.

If the salaried employee is the customer, what is the product? I believe there are only two broad categories of automation services: custom systems and standard vehicles.

Information professionals have been building custom data processing systems for 30 years. Each one has been a specific solution to a functional or individual need, with all the attendant problems of limited life, costly maintenance, and general dissatisfaction with the disparities between what the customer wanted and what he or she got.

An alternative to custom-designed systems is a standard vehicle, which is a general solution to an information problem presented in a sufficiently friendly fashion for the individual to assume personal responsibility for it. The spreadsheet approach to presenting and analyzing financial data as embodied in Visicalc is a classic example of a standard vehicle. Of course, standard vehicles have their own problems of documentation, standardization, and control.

To get a custom solution a user specifies requirements to an information system analyst, who proceeds to build a custom product. This can be called systems development. By planning for the conception, birth, growth, maturity, and death of the product over a life cycle, systems development explicitly recognizes the obsolescence of the custom solution. By contrast, with a standard vehicle the user is educated into a solution without having to master the mysteries of electronic data processing. The educating is done by a professional who becomes the coach, informs the user of corporate standards, and helps select the best technology to satisfy the user's information needs.

At Reynolds we started with the assumption that eventually every salaried employee will have a terminal. Every terminal will be tied to a network, and that network can access any computer. Although this is not something we can afford to do today, at least we have defined the problem, we know how to solve it, and it will become cheap enough to implement in the future. It may cost twice as much today to deliver a given service automatically as it does to deliver it manually, but if our cost projections hold true, crossover occurs in two years, after which automation is less expensive.

Users will bear the cost of the terminal and a pro rata cost for using the network. We assume they will justify those devices based on productivity improvements of the staff. Other possible justifications include better service or new kinds of service that could not be provided in any other fashion. But the focus is on productivity.

To determine what kinds of automation would be needed we began by identifying six delivery vehicles for automated information processing: word processing, electronic mail, data inquiry, transaction processing, technical computation, and business analysis. We then took the personnel system's function codes for all salaried employees and mapped them against the six delivery vehicles to identify the size of the market for each vehicle.

Secretaries can obviously use word processing, but the market segment for this vehicle is much larger. Lawyers are wordsmiths; programmers and systems analysts are in the business of language translation; and public relations and purchasing departments already have word processing capabilities. We currently have over 400 terminals providing word processing support. Essentially, what they do is format and edit words, but these capabilities can easily be expanded. Add technical computation and business analysis, and not just words but an entire report can be formated. Wrap an electronic envelope around a memo or a report, plug it into electronic mail, and it can be delivered to the recipient.

Only managers are considered an appropriate market for electronic mail. Among the things managers do is send and receive a lot of memos. Electronic mail appears to be a fine vehicle for sending, receiving, and following up on memos. Currently Reynolds has over two dozen terminals that are sending and receiving memos by electronic mail. This includes a few intended primarily for international communications. Automatic follow-up, scheduling, and calendaring routines are available.

Data inquiry services are "marketed" to employees who need access to public information or large data banks. In 1980 we had only a handful of terminals justified for this purpose. To determine who needed what kinds of data we brought in a data dictionary, which allows users to define the information they need to access. To meet these needs we have bought two language-processing systems: INQUIRE and INTELLECT.

INQUIRE is a text-processing language with very powerful Boolean logic capabilities. Our research librarians find it an effective tool for abstracting, storing, and retrieving information about company reports and projects. The same language is being developed for use by the legal department to store abstracts of legal contracts and maintain an index of where those contracts are physically stored.

INTELLECT is a parsing program that analyzes an English sentence typed on a computer terminal and generates a call to a specific database. The first application of INTELLECT has been in support of our Human Resource Development (HRD) search activity.

In addition to database and query-language facilities, the System/38, with its own capabilities, is providing outstanding service and accounts for the largest segment of our recent growth in the area of data inquiry. Further, we are just becoming comfortable with the database tool on the personal computer.

I expect that as we become proficient in defining data for these kinds of systems anyone who has a terminal will be able to use data inquiry to get access to needed information. Data inquiry will largely supplant printed reports as the vehicle for distributing information from automated systems.

Transaction processing is our largest delivery vehicle. In three years this application has grown 50 percent to over 900 terminals that support clerks who enter and process transactions. All terminals now exercise systems built to process transactions in a conventional manner. We have defined a requirement to handle the other 5,000 forms that the company is currently processing manually. We are now seeking a universal form processor that will allow a user to call up on a terminal any form used in the company, fill in the blanks, and send it by electronic mail to the individual or computer that has to review it, approve it, or process it. If this capability is acquired, we believe it would be used by almost everyone.

Technical computation is used by our technicians, engineers, and scientists. Timesharing has been the delivery vehicle, and the applications are mainly specialized routines the company has purchased or the users have written for themselves.

Business analysis was the final delivery vehicle we identified. In many companies business analysts, planners, accountants, and others have long used automation as a vehicle for improving their productivity. At the beginning of 1980, however, Reynolds had no terminals to support such individuals. This situation has changed with the availability of color graphics and analytic tool packages. A spreadsheet computer program such as Visicalc, which runs on a personal computer, is very popular; we wish it were available now on larger IBM machines. When it is we believe the number of terminals used by business analysts will grow even more rapidly.

How is the investment in various automation delivery vehicles justified? I have already explained that in order to determine the market for each of the six delivery vehicles we mapped the number of people in each functional job code against their potential to use a primary delivery vehicle. The resulting match-up was also used for justification purposes.

Obviously, we expect most users to employ more than one delivery vehicle. For example, secretaries who primarily use word processing also process transactions and inquire into databases. But the justification for this investment requires an improvement in productivity that is usually assumed to be measurable only by the primary focus. Once a terminal is installed for primary access, of course, other delivery vehicles can be made available.

When we matched job functions with delivery vehicles we found that terminals for about 57 percent of the salaried employees would be justified by transaction processing. The second largest justified use (15 percent) was for technical computation. This is because Reynolds is a manufacturing and technology company and has a significant cadre of engineers and scientists. Three percent of the staff was identified as managers, and should have devices justified for electronic mail. The balance was about evenly split between word processing (10 percent), database (9 percent), and business analysis (6 percent).

Quite a different picture emerged when we looked at the actual use of delivery vehicles compared to the justified (or projected) use. (See Figure 2.) The productivity improvement in one primary area had provided the justification, but microcomputers are in fact blurring the lines between vehicles, causing changes in job function and rebalancing the workload. What seems to be happening is that automation is changing the jobs of salaried employees.

The individual delivery vehicles have had widely varying growth rates between 1980 and 1983. Transaction processing, which began with the largest base, has been growing steadily at about 15 percent per year. Technical computation doubled in 1980 and grew another 60 percent during 1981. Word processing more than doubled in each of its first three years and is approaching 50 percent penetration of the market. In all, these three vehicles should satisfy over 80 percent of Reynolds's automation needs when fully implemented.

Data inquiry, business analysis, and electronic mail began the decade at ground zero. In the last two years, both data inquiry and business analysis have broken out of the pilot/test modes and have achieved market acceptance. Electronic mail has not been as successful, and research is now under way to find out why.

With its market reasonably defined and delivery vehicles in place, Reynolds addressed the issue of the rates of growth we could manage while meeting our end-of-the-decade objective. As a percentage of our salaried work force, individuals using automation grew from a base of 6 percent at the start of 1979 to 21 percent in January 1983. A compound growth rate of 30 percent per year from 1983 on would achieve the 1990 objective of 100 percent automation. Actual growth has been over 33 percent per year, compounded. As productivity improvements are achieved the salaried work force needed to handle a given volume of business is being reduced. This makes 100 percent automation delivery by 1990 even more likely.

Along with the marketing and growth aspects of its long-term plan, Reynolds has identified a number of organizational issues that demand attention. These can be broadly divided into technology, management, and cultural issues.

Computers are available in a dazzling variety of sizes, capabili-

JUSTIFIED USE

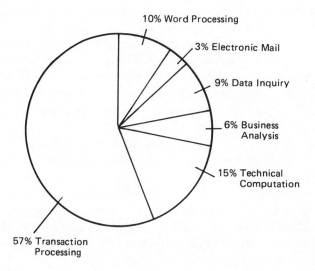

ACTUAL USE

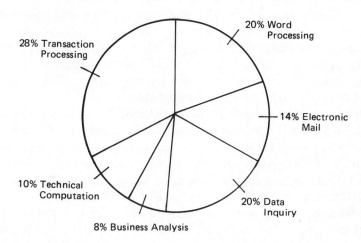

FIGURE 2   Justified versus actual use of automation delivery vehicles by Reynolds Metals salaried employees.

ties, and costs. To deal with this diverse technology Reynolds simplified its perception to three sizes: large, medium, and small. Two large Amdahls manage the corporate information systems and interconnect all other machines. Medium-sized IBM System/ 38s manage plant and department information needs. The IBM Displaywriter and personal computers provide individual automation capability. All of these machines are connected through a network. Although some form of each delivery vehicle capability is currently available on all user devices, some are better than others. The long-term objective is for all user devices to provide high levels of all six automation functions.

To successfully change the mode of distributed processing in a company (that is, to change from manual to automated processing throughout), the three key variables of hardware, software, and management must be organized in some way. The question is—how? If we simplify the possible operating environment for each of these variables to either totally centralized or totally decentralized, a number of combinations are possible. These can be viewed as the eight corners of a cube (Figure 3).

For example, centralized electronic data processing (EDP) functions best when all three variables (hardware, software, and management) are centralized. At the opposite extreme is the personal computer, with all three variables totally decentralized.

At the back plane of the cube in Figure 3, where management is centralized, three combinations are possible. If only software is relaxed (decentralized), development is distributed. Alternatively, relaxing hardware leads to distributed processing. Decentralizing both hardware and software with centralized management requires strong efforts toward standardization.

The face plane represents decentralized management. If this occurs when hardware and software are both centralized, frustration is the usual result. When hardware remains centralized and software is relaxed, timesharing and remote job entry are the result. Centralizing hardware and relaxing software are equivalent to purchasing packages.

Most organizations consist of some mix of all or most of the eight extremes of automated processing. The important point is for organizations to know where they stand and where they are likely to be in the future.

The culture of an organization poses a final set of concerns for automation efforts. Although it is unplotted in Figure 3, a culture

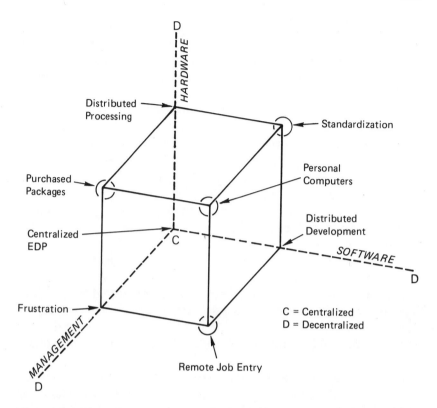

FIGURE 3   Operating space of automated information processing.

is present in every company. The culture of an organization must change as it moves through the hardware-software-management cube. In general, I believe that automation professionals need to reorient themselves from custom systems to standard solutions. This frees key personnel to become coaches and focuses a smaller cadre on technology planning, evaluation, and selection. Other employees need to accept automation education, devices, and networks that give access to information. This allows individuals to accept responsibility for their own information requirements.

A comparison of the cultural implications of automation with those of human resources clarifies the management issue. Along with money and machines, people and information are resources every organization must manage. The personnel function is recognized by most organizations as a key one, and reports are made to the chief executive officer or one step below. Well-run personnel departments provide expertise in recruiting, compensation, development, evaluation, and training. However, *management* of the human resources is not the responsibility of the personnel department but of managers at various department and section levels.

Information management should be considered in the same light. For too long it has been delegated to the EDP or MIS department. Yet computers are no more complex to manage than people. Every manager and information worker needs to understand what information is needed, where it is, who controls it, how good it is, and how to get it. Plans to improve information availability, cut costs, and measure performance should be made annually, just like human resource development plans.

How to make people recognize that information management is part of every manager's job is another question. Leadership needs to come from the information systems ranks. Identifying the chairman, president, or business unit vice-president who will be the role model in the organization is essential. Articles in periodicals such as the *Harvard Business Review*, *Fortune*, and *Business Week*, which popularize the role of information management, will also be helpful.

Reynolds has given priority to four technical issues. First, we need a data dictionary that spans the full range of automation devices from personal computers to departmental machines to corporate mainframes. The second issue is access. Once we know what information is located where, access must be available to all who need it. The access issue leads directly to privacy and security issues. Information must be available only to those who should have it, and in a fashion that assures individual privacy.

The fourth technical issue involves optimal selection of devices and networks. Presently we analyze stated needs and select the best devices to meet these needs. We then build networks to connect the devices. A better approach would be to feed all sources and uses of data to a model that provides the best combination and use of computers, terminals, and networks.

On the management side of the equation, we have identified a number of difficult open issues. One of the major issues we will face, both as individuals and as organizations, is how to implement productivity improvements. If a group of 10 clerks increases its productivity by 50 percent, a fairly straightforward management response would be to allow turnover or reduction in the work force. However, if a marketing manager or an engineering manager is given a device that doubles productivity, it is much more difficult to decide how to take advantage of it. Do you give the marketing manager two markets to manage? Do you give the engineering manager both engineering and marketing to manage?

It will be a major challenge for the management of Reynolds and other companies to find ways to restructure jobs to take advantage of the improvements in productivity made possible by automation. Inevitably, some people will be displaced. Managers in our company and the country at large are going to have to address the issue of retraining these people.

A second management issue we are now facing in the course of increasing security for corporate data is the question of who owns what data. Reynolds has bought a sophisticated computer program that requires identifying who owns each piece of data, who can access it, who can change it, and who can delete it. This raises some interesting questions. For example, does a piece of tax information in a division system belong to the tax department or to the division?

A third issue involves measuring productivity. Economic feasibility has been blithely assumed, but it needs to be tested at every point. On the one hand, Reynolds has established a goal to double the productivity of its salaried work force. On the other, we don't even measure the productivity of our salaried work force today. We can measure the ratio of the total number of salaried employees to pounds of aluminum or dollars of sales. On an individual basis, however, we don't know what productivity is and we don't know how to measure it. I believe this question of how to measure individual productivity is an issue we will wrestle with at least for the rest of the decade.

A final management issue involves multiple functions and responsibilities. In the past auditors have taken a lot of comfort in the careful separation of responsibility. One person requisitions a purchase, a second approves, a third receives, and a fourth pays the invoice. Automation makes it possible for a single individual to perform more than one function. Reynold's management, as well as its auditors, must consider what kinds of controls to build into automated information processing systems. These controls must provide adequate protection for corporate assets, assure proper processing of financial transactions, and at the same time achieve the necessary improvements in productivity.

I think the broad conclusions to be drawn from Reynolds' efforts are clear and important. First, information processing is just too important a component of every salaried employee's job to subcontract it to information specialists or anyone else. It needs to be a part of each employee's job description.

Second, the decreasing cost of automation technology and the increasing cost of people will not only permit but will mandate that every salaried employee's productivity be improved through the use of automated technology during the course of this decade.

Third, redesigning jobs to take advantage of the productivity potential provided by automation is going to present major challenges to management in this decade.

Microcomputers are machines. Like all machines they have advantages and disadvantages. To deal with them successfully organizations need an automation strategy, an understanding of how microcomputers fit, an automation plan, and a mechanism to monitor performance.

Reynolds is only one company that has begun this process. I believe that all firms that successfully automate their information functions will develop a competitive edge over those that do not.

Managing Microcomputers in State and Local Government

*Fred Dugger**

State and local governments, like private sector companies, face a new and formidable challenge—how to harness the technology of powerful, inexpensive microcomputers to improve the organization's productivity. The computing power and low cost of these devices are well known. What is not as well known is how to manage their prudent use. We must initially identify areas where productivity might be improved by using micros. Then we must address issues of product selection, procurement procedures, software acquisition and development, communications network integration, education, and maintenance. We must determine how microcomputer technology can enhance rather than confuse our information generating systems. We must distribute computing power throughout our organizations while maintaining the necessary information flow to top management. And we must accomplish this in an environment so dynamic that tomorrow's product announcements may make yesterday's requests for bids obsolete.

This dynamic environment extends to users and potential users as well. It seems that almost everyone has a strong, sometimes

*Fred Dugger is director of the Department of Data Processing, State of Nevada (Carson City).

highly emotional opinion about micros and personal computers. People who own them often consider them a friend; their children almost always do. These people believe that micros have a definite place in their own office environment. They are probably right.

Other people with little or no direct contact with micros are still intrigued. The media have brought home the fact that ours is a computerized society; our children have frequent access to computers at school; Dick Cavett, Charlie Chaplin, and Captain Kirk have shown us how we can generate sophisticated graphics for our businesses with a single keystroke. And with the plummeting price of hardware how can we afford *not* to install one? There is surely a sales rep at the other end of the telephone who can solve all our problems.

Then there are the professionals in traditional data processing organizations who have sweated blood for so many years developing, installing, and maintaining enormous, highly sophisticated systems. These systems perform large-scale accounting operations, transfer millions of dollars daily around the country, and provide countless other services in government and the private sector. Will these organizations lose the power they have acquired, the talent they have gathered? If they no longer control computer acquisitions, will the chaos of the early days return in the form of unmaintainable systems; programs written by authors who have long vanished, unstructured, unplanned systems; communications incompatibilities; a complete lack of documentation?

Finally, there is the largest group of all, the uneasy white-collar workers who believe they will have to embrace this new and strange technology, master it instantly, and improve productivity measurably while continuing to cope with everything they are now barely able to accomplish. These people know that they will soon have to alter fundamentally and permanently the way in which they accomplish their day-to-day tasks. They know that change means stress. And they are worried.

So what do we do? Do we even have a choice? Can we opt to refuse the new technology, to continue with methods that now appear to be at the peak of efficiency? The answer is no. We have no choice on whether micros will be in our organizations. We do have a choice as to how they will be controlled, acquired, supported and, in general, put to productive use.

But how do we measure productive use? The answer is economics, pure and simple. Unfortunately, in all too many cases the mystique of computers has successfully evaded cost-benefit analyses and return on investment calculations. There is no reason for this. Computers are tools, and data processing centers are machine shops. The same economics apply. Data processing "experts" may attempt the standard technique of claiming independence from accountability due to technical complexity, but this is no excuse. As with every other capital and operating cost, line managers must be responsible for the costs associated with implementation and use of micros.

It is only fair, however, to make sure that managers understand the true costs of microcomputers. Usually, the major cost of a microcomputer lies in the cost of the people who program and operate it. It is this consumption of personnel resource that is almost always underestimated, particularly if it involves any original programming. Functions that have been performed in traditional data processing applications are often completely ignored by people acquiring new microcomputers. As a result, those who attempt to write programs without systems planning, analysis, design, and data definition are doomed to commit the disastrous errors that plagued the early data processing industry. One can only hope these disasters will be on a smaller scale.

The economics, then, are simple: equipment is cheap, people are expensive. Minimize people requirements. Eliminate programming by buying off-the-shelf software. Minimize training time by providing a helpful support staff. Standardize vendors, both hardware and software, for common applications. Provide centralized maintenance wherever possible. Provide an internal qualified consultant staff to answer the myriad questions on common micros and associated software that will arise from first-time users.

In short, make micros easy to use. If they are easy to use they require less staff time, and that means less money.

What have state and local governments done to facilitate the use of microcomputers? The answer is—many things. States' responses to the microcomputer onslaught have been as varied as their existing data processing organizational structures. Those with highly centralized data processing authorities and procurement agencies quickly developed new policies and procedures to cover micros. Authorization procedures tended to stress proof of beneficial use, as well as sources of funding and cost-benefit analyses. Those organizations that already had approval authority for data processing applications and equipment also exercised approval authority for microcomputers. Standardized forms for requesting micros have been implemented in many organizations. In a similar fashion, centralized purchasing authorities developed qualified vendor lists, negotiated volume discount agreements, and published procedures to be used to request microcomputer equipment.

Some government agencies have modified their organizational structure to accommodate new demands. The state of Kentucky has created a new unit within its systems services branch called the Microcomputer Support Unit (MSU). This unit has been directed to establish policies concerning the evaluation and use of microcomputers by Kentucky state government, and to provide technical, financial, contractual, and management support for these policies. The unit has developed forms for mini-microcomputer needs assessments and cost-benefit analyses. These new forms, along with preexisting ones, provide a way to determine the suitability of a proposed microcomputer installation. The MSU also coordinates all activity with microcomputer vendors on behalf of the state; initiates all hardware and software purchases; and registers all software, whether developed in-house or purchased. Although the unit does not itself provide software development services, the MSU will coordinate with the information systems department to provide that service if custom software is needed.

The Kentucky Microcomputer Support Unit has the additional responsibility of developing and implementing standards and guidelines for hardware and software acquisition. The MSU has established a recommended list of software packages, specific to the applications desired, and has set standard communications protocols for micros that communicate with mainframe computers. The unit is developing guidelines to make installation and operation of microcomputers easier, including suggestions on backup and recovery procedures. The MSU is also developing an internal "computer store." This store will have an inventory of approved microcomputers, peripheral devices, and software in common use. This equipment may be borrowed by state agencies for short-term use and is available for demonstrations and tests. The store is expected to facilitate comparisons of various micros and software packages, and prospective purchasers will be able to solicit advice from objective, rather than sales-oriented, staff. Finally, the MSU will serve as a clearinghouse for all application programs, provide advice on career training for microcomputer users, run a hotline service for questions, and coordinate all equipment maintenance and service.

Clearly, Kentucky is taking an approach that will facilitate selection, use, and maintenance of microcomputers while maintaining procurement and authorization controls and procedures. The state's investment in staffing the MSU will be recovered many times over in the time savings of the personnel supported. The creation of this organizational structure reflects management's commitment to the effective use of microcomputers.

The state of California has long been noted for its centralized control over acquisition of data processing equipment and procurement procedures. California has formulated a central policy for microcomputer acquisition as well, but has left procurement authority for such equipment with the various data processing entities throughout the state. Several of these departments have developed their own guidelines for selecting microcomputers. The Health and Welfare Department has implemented the computer store concept for its internal use. Members of this department may make an appointment to visit the store to discuss their computing requirements with data processing staff. On display and available for trial use are microcomputers that are compatible with department mainframes. Quantity discount arrangements have been made with various vendors through the California central purchasing authority. The computer store has been so popular that it has had to restrict access to only its own department staff. Other departments are watching this approach and are considering stores of their own. California is continuing to develop centralized policies for other aspects of microcomputer use, and is currently investigating ways of providing equipment maintenance. The state does not now have a centralized education capability for microcomputer users and is also quite concerned about mainframe compatibility.

Other governments have implemented other methods of control. The state of Illinois reviews each request for microcomputer acquisition against the master data processing plan for the requesting agency. If the microcomputer performs a service that supports the plan, and if it is economically beneficial, it receives approval. If the acquisition does not support the plan, the purchase is either disapproved or the plan is changed and subsequent approval is sought. Dade County, Florida, has placed its micro-computer support function within the data processing organizations in its Information Center. The Information Center has already been providing support for user-friendly software on large mainframes, attempting to bring hands-on computer power directly to analytical and managerial personnel without requiring traditional computer programming. The information center concept has achieved widespread success. Dade County believes that the user orientation of the Information Center staff will help establish correct use of microcomputers. The center also provides an excellent opportunity to compare directly the capabilities of applications software running on large mainframes and on personal computers.

The state of Alaska is pursuing a policy that attempts to avoid duplication of mainframe functions on microcomputers. The state recognizes that there are substantial differences in information systems requirements, and that much time and effort can be wasted trying to shoehorn a large application into a small computer in the name of efficiency. Like Kentucky, Alaska is standardizing off-the-shelf software packages for specific applications, thereby improving the mobility of experienced staff and reducing training requirements. The state has also developed its own training courses and materials. In one rather innovative program Alaska is using prelaw students to assist in developing applications programs to support legislative functions. The students receive university credit for their work.

Several other states have taken less comprehensive approaches. These are understandable if we keep in mind that, in general, state governments more closely resemble a collection of independent companies, each with a unique set of goals, rather than a single large company with an overall profit objective. In other words, providing drivers' licenses has little to do with licensing real estate brokers, except that both must be accomplished at the lowest cost to the taxpayer and with the highest quality of service. As a result of the disparate functions of state agencies, decisions about acquisition and use of microcomputers are frequently left to the individual agency. Since most agencies do not have the resources to provide specialized internal consulting for microcomputers, those that want to take advantage of the new technology must fend for themselves. This has sometimes led to a proliferation of microcomputer vendors, software products, and limited communications capability. It has also consumed a great deal of personnel resource, as people who are unfamiliar with microcomputers visit computer stores and attend seminars and expositions to increase their technical knowledge. Perhaps the worst consequence is the frustration and disillusionment of managers who must struggle with the consequences of buying the wrong computer for a task or must use novice programmers to try to build customized software.

The state of Washington's Employment Security Department (ESD) offers a good example of a department-level approach to microcomputers. ESD has developed a microcomputer-based system to support its Job Placement Training Act (JPTA) activities. This application involves a local area networking system that allows cross-communication between sites and communication to the ESD mainframe. Insofar as local area networking is much talked about but little understood these days, several other states are watching the developments in Washington with great interest. Some of these states, including Nevada, have entered into agreements with Washington to allow transfer of the contractor-developed software to their own JPTA programs. Many interesting issues are surfacing during these transfers, and it appears that the operation of the Washington system and the transfers to other states will provide excellent learning opportunities.

In Nevada current planning strategy distinguishes between backbone systems, which are information systems considered vital to the effective operation of an organization, and decision support systems, which provide digested information to management and program personnel. Examples of backbone systems include payroll, corporation licensing, gaming tax and license fee collection, and motor vehicle registration. Decision support systems include caseload projections, revenue projections, and tax impact analysis. Professional data processing personnel will continue to develop, implement, and maintain the state's backbone systems, thereby utilizing the most expensive resource, people, to insure the quality of the most valuable asset, timely and accurate data. The new technologies of the improved, user-friendly software products and microcomputers, functioning as professional workstations, will provide direct computing power to managers and analysts.

State governments as a group, functioning through the National Association of State Information Systems (NASIS), have recognized the magnitude of the management problem they face. They have accepted as a primary responsibility the development of policies, procedures, and techniques to make the best use of the new microcomputer technology. They have also recognized that all states have similar, if not identical, problems. In an effort to share ideas and resources and to cooperate in solving common problems, NASIS has established an Information Clearinghouse. This clearinghouse will function as a common repository for states' policies, procedures, plans, productivity techniques, and anything else that might help achieve excellence in information systems services. Although few documents are currently indexed and stored, the Research and Education Committee of NASIS has placed a major emphasis on acquiring and indexing quality documents from the states. NASIS wishes to extend the availability of these documents beyond its membership to other governmental entities and to the private sector. Mechanisms are now being developed to allow distribution of an index of available documents, as well as the documents themselves.

It is too soon to evaluate the approaches of various state and local governments to managing microcomputers within their organizations. Based on some of their early experiences, however, it is possible to make some recommendations about the use of microcomputers by government and private sector organizations:

• Recognize that microcomputers are becoming an increasingly important tool for your professional staff. Micros are here to stay.

• Provide management support for a cohesive microcomputer policy in your organization.

• Establish an organizational unit that understands microcomputers and can provide quality advice for internal management. Such a unit can cut through marketing claims and provide realistic assessments of capabilities.

• Use your established expertise in systems engineering. An organization's data processing professionals can greatly facilitate an integrated systems approach using the new low-cost hardware.

• Monitor early microcomputer installations closely. Capitalize on the successes and learn from the failures.

• Provide for and insist on education for your management

staff. They don't have to understand how computers work, but they must understand their capabilities and limitations.

• Do not expect microcomputers to replace the large information systems currently in place on mainframes. Properly managed, micros can provide valuable local support functions while enhancing the quality and quantity of the corporate database. Improperly managed, micros can diffuse the database and confuse the accuracy of data.

Although the challenge of managing the microcomputer invasion appears large, the opportunities that micros provide are also enormous. The power and flexibility they bring will permit quantum leaps in the provision of quality information. These thinking robots are amplifying the analytical power our organizations possess at a cost undreamed of a decade ago. As we learn how to harness this new technology we will be able to use its powerful capabilities to achieve our goals better, faster, and more economically.

The User Era

Martin B. Zimmerman*

In the late 1970s Richard Nolan described a six-stage model for the evolution of computers and information systems (*Harvard Business Review*, March–April 1978). This model provides a framework for the U.S. Army's present initiatives in automation. A brief description of the model will help clarify the motivation behind these initiatives.

Stage 1: Initiation. The first use of computers in most organizations was to solve well-defined problems and to unburden those involved in repetitive functions such as payroll and accounting. For the U.S. Army this occurred during the period 1956–1962.

Stage 2: Expansion. This stage was characterized by an explosion in the use of computer technology. Hardware was king. Little was known of the software problem. Computers were placed behind glass walls and the uninitiated were paraded past the mysterious devices in semireligious ceremonies. Companies and organizations depended on the computer industry for total system solutions in what were described as "turnkey" systems contracts. This second stage can best be described by its laissez-faire

*Martin B. Zimmerman is deputy assistant, deputy chief of staff for operations and plans, U.S. Army, where he serves as technical advisor on automation.

management and decentralized decision making. The result was "good news and bad news." The bad news was that decentralized management led to the development of duplicate functional systems. The Army, for example, had 49 automated payroll systems in 1968. The good news was that without such an expansion stage the industry would not have been able to develop the corporate professionals required for subsequent phases of growth. The uncontrolled nature of the expansion naturally led to the next stage.

Stage 3: Control. In this stage steering committees were established, budgetary control procedures developed, and central design agencies organized. Technological talent was concentrated within the organization, and companies believed they could solve all their own problems. Development using in-house assets was in; contractual support was out. This stage resulted in users' frustration caused by the inability of central development departments to solve *all* user problems.

Stage 4: Integration. This stage is characterized by increased interactivity, data management, and management initiatives to integrate information horizontally. The concept of developing a corporate database and sharing information among corporate staff is inherent in stage 4. A return to decentralization also marks this stage, since more systems are user-developed. Nolan, in fact, believes that stages 1–3 can be categorized as the "era of the computer," while stages 4–6 can be defined as the "era of the user."

Stage 5: Data Ownership. This stage is characterized by the need to assign data ownership and a focus on solving the natural friction between the data processing professional and the increasingly literate and active user.

Stage 6: Maturity. This final stage occurs when organizations are experienced enough to design a corporate planning model derived from corporate databases.

Today, most organizations are moving out of stage 3, central control, and into stage 4, integration—from the end of the computer era to the beginning of the user era. Three phenomena are stimulating this move.

The first phenomenon can be called limits to the design activity. The software factories of the late 1960s and early 1970s were established to solve most if not all software development problems. They have not, however, succeeded as envisioned. As systems developed and proliferated more users were trained. Over time these users requested more and more changes to the basic systems. Such changes, part of the software "maintenance" process, have used up 70 percent of the in-house programing resources of most organizations. Unfortunately, this does not mean that 30 percent of the corporate programing staff will always be available for new functions. A hypothetical example shows why: If an organization began development of a system with 1,000 programmer/analysts, at the end of the effort 700 would remain for maintenance and 300 would be available to develop a second system. This second design activity, when finished would require 210 personnel (70 percent) for maintenance, leaving only 90 programmer/analysts for the third system. It is obvious from this example that the number of systems any single organization can both develop and maintain is finite. And user frustration is the ultimate result.

The second phenomenon is increased user literacy. For more than 20 years computers represented a mysterious technology, understood only by data processing professionals. Today, however, computers are everywhere, and computer literacy, aided by software products that permit unique system development without the need to understand COBOL, FORTRAN, or any other high order language, has greatly increased.

The third phenomenon that has spurred movement out of the control stage is the technology explosion. The cost performance curve in logical devices has led to a sizable expansion in their use. If we continue to acquire computers in the future at the same rate as we have in the past, we will compound deliveries at 25 percent annually. Theoretically, computer growth requires an equivalent expansion in trained programmers. Today there are 300,000 programmers. By one estimate, approximately 3 million would be needed by 1994 to maintain the current computer-to-programmer ratio. Since such expansion is unlikely, greater dependence must by placed on the user community. Fortunately, the software industry has the capability to help solve the problem.

The dynamics of change in the information industry and society's continuing thirst for technology-aided solutions demand responses from organizational management. One user of computer technology, the U.S. Department of the Army, has identified seven initiatives to help deal with information systems:

1. Establish a single management source. The Army is in the process of creating a new corporate "officer" who will provide central control for planning, programing, policy setting, and developing resources for all facets of information systems (the information itself, automation, and communication facilities).

2. Establish a single developer for critical nonbattlefield information systems. This concept does not conflict with the plan to involve the user community in a major portion of future systems developments. It does recognize, however, that some systems are so complex that they can only be developed by professional programmers. Further, systems developed by the individual user become candidates for organizational standardization. The central developer ultimately becomes responsible for the "maintenance" of systems selected for such standardization.

3. Emphasize technology. In an attempt to seek homogeneous technological solutions, thus minimizing software development costs, the Army has acquired or is in the process of acquiring a variety of hardware and software that will support this effort. It includes standardized minicomputers and a family of microcomputers; a set of hardware and supporting software that satisfies the department's worldwide administrative and mobilization information needs; a broad-band local area network within the Pentagon to integrate multifunctional information needs; video teleconferencing technology to be installed initially at 18 locations, with options for additional installations; and a Data Base Management System (DBMS) for use on one vendor's standard mainframes. The Army has also begun efforts to develop a software package that will combine the best features of relational, network, and hierarchical DBMS techniques.

4. Improve planning. Nolan articulated the need to develop horizontal corporate database systems in lieu of the present vertical, single-function systems. To do this requires a unique analytical method. IBM, among a limited number of companies, has developed a procedure called Information Systems Planning (ISP) that details the steps required in such an analysis. The Army has adopted the method and is in the process of performing ISP studies worldwide.

5. Develop a new technologist. The melding of communication

and automation technologies demands individuals skilled in both fields. The Army is engaged in developing programs that will train such persons.

6. Define the relative roles of users and data processing professionals. The increase in the ability of users to perform their own data processing functions has led to friction between these two groups. Yet both need to play key roles. Specifically, the professional should: design, develop, and manage the common user network; develop software that satisfies the needs of more than one agency or activity, such as payroll and budget; develop and enforce standards throughout the organization; establish and staff the organization's information center, which instructs users on new tools; provide fourth-generation software tools; and act as the database administrator, ensuring that every data element has a single owner who has identified procedures for its use. Finally, this professional should develop a procedure to provide visibility for user-developed software. The Army has developed a software clearinghouse that will function in two ways. Users can find out if software already exists that meets their requirements before initiating new development. Professionals can use the clearinghouse to identify software products that are candidates for standardization.

7. Establish standards. In the public sector establishing standards is the only real way to ensure both economic and effective systems development. Although the computer industry has defined standards in certain areas, it has not formulated standards in other areas for purely business reasons. The Army has set its own standards in five broad areas:

Languages.   COBOL, FORTRAN, BASIC and Ada (for battlefield systems) are established standards. SIMSCRIPT, LISP, C, and PASCAL are other languages that have been used for specific and obvious functions.

Data Base Management Systems (DBMS).   The Army has a variety of DBMSs. On most of its large IBM mainframes, DATACOM D/B is used. For the future the Army believes that the solution lies in the creation of a simple but standard data manipulation language. The software behind the language could be developed to manage databases using hierarchical, network, or relational procedures. With such a solution present databases could be preserved.

Communication protocols. The Army is committed to the Defense Data Network (DDN) protocols (based on the seven-layer reference standard of the International Organization for Standardization). Systems that do not satisfy DDN will not be purchased.

Operating systems. The Army will establish as preferred standards CP/M for 8-bit micros and both UNIX (version V) and MS DOS for 16/32 bit-micros, with UNIX preferred.

Local area networks. The Army will initially use ETHERNET protocols (CSMA/CD), but recognizes that it is probably too early in the development of this technology to commit to a single standard.

Without doubt, society is in the midst of major change in its use of computer technology. Clearly, the seminal force is the availability of ever more powerful technology at relatively low cost. Computer literacy has increased at an exponential rate. The pressure on the software industry for more software products for the professional has exceeded its capability to respond. However, the industry has made specific user-oriented software products available.

To shape a program that benefits from these varied forces the Army has chosen to provide top-down planning and broad architecture; bottom-up, user-initiated development; a procedure for giving visibility to user-developed software; a definition of the relative roles of the professional and the user; and a set of preferred standards to increase compatibility and minimize the cost of software. The specific course of action the Army has chosen will clearly be iterative.

In nineteenth-century England a band of workmen known as Luddites tried to prevent the use of labor-saving machinery by destroying it. Obviously, this was not a very successful response to technological change. Managing today's computer technology also requires the ability to implement change appropriately. Those organizations that remain static will be the Luddites of tomorrow.

Personal Computing, Not Personal Computers

*Norman M. Epstein**

At E.F. Hutton we do not believe in personal computers, but we do believe in personal computing. This is more than a semantic difference. It affects the technology applied, the philosophy we adhere to, and the planning that went into our system.

Although we think our approach is a very obvious and logical one, apparently others do not. It reminds me of the famous story of Louis Pasteur and the maggots. In Pasteur's day people believed that maggots came from decaying meat because every place there was decaying meat there were maggots. But Pasteur, being a scientist, took decaying meat, put it in a large bell jar, and covered the bell jar with gauze. He came back three days later and found the maggots on top of the gauze, proving that maggots came from gauze.

In short, the system has to suit you. And if you look around, no one is wearing the same suit. Our organization would seem to be a perfect candidate for personal computers. We have 400 branch offices around the world and a campus in lower Manhattan with 6,000 people in 12 buildings. We have 9,000 people in the field, 6,000 account executives, and 3,000 people in support positions.

Our goal has been to automate the operation in the field. There-

---

*Norman M. Epstein is executive vice-president and director of E.F. Hutton Group and E.F. Hutton and Company, Inc., New York, New York.

fore, our approach might not work for a company with 14,000 people in one building.

Currently, each of our 6,000 account executives has a single terminal on a desk. These terminals are called branch information-processing system terminals (BIPs). The terminal comes out of a dual-port CPU (central processing unit), and data comes from two different networks, Bunker Ramo and our own.

When our system is complete everyone in the firm except telephone operators and porters will have a terminal. Everyone. The multipurpose use of this terminal is the most important aspect of our system. We have a limited amount of space on a desk, and we are going to accommodate it by having one terminal. That one terminal may be supplied by Data General, by IBM, by Wang, by Bunker Ramo. But no matter who makes it, each terminal will have access into all the databases. The secondary function of each terminal determines the reason for selecting a particular product. For example, the Bunker Ramo terminal is selected because it is a market data system, the Wang terminal because it has certain word processing capabilities, the Data General terminal because it ties into our operations and communications.

How are our operations and communications tied together? We start with head-end computers that create the databases and supply information at corporate headquarters. The next level down consists of about 35 Data General Eclipses located at regional offices around the world. Why do we have a distributed network around the world? Most people involved with personal computing know that when you hit the button and have to wait any length of time for a response, you're in trouble. The reason for the distributed network is very simple: hit the button, get a response. Obviously, when the computer is in the branch you can talk much faster.

This part of the system provides only the data. There is nothing fancy about the technology, no state-of-the-art breakthroughs. We have simply recognized that if having data in a central location does not give adequate response time economically, we must move the data out.

At the next level is the branch information processing system. It is the integrated architecture of the network. It consists of 400 Data General MV-4000s, one in each branch. The MV-4000 is larger than the computer that ran all of E.F. Hutton's communications a dozen years ago. It is basically a 2-megabyte machine, .6

MIPS (mega-instructions per second), and 350 million characters of storage. This is an awesome box, and it is sitting in a branch office. The terminal hangs off this box, with high-speed, dual mode printers and a local database for very rapid response time and for personal computing.

At the bottom of the hierarchy, the terminal level, the branch information processing system has the ability to grow whereas the personal computer does not. And the system can grow in the same box, for the terminals do not need to change. They are essentially just a light bulb and a screen. The brains of that terminal sits in the branch office. We estimate that one MV-4000 can accommodate 30 or 35 terminals. And, in general, we have three terminals to one letter quality printer.

These levels—headquarters, region, branch, and terminal—are the fabric of our communications and data processing capability, and they are all interconnected. The host complex controls the distributed information system and the distributed information system controls the branch processing. Users can reach around it or through it to get to whatever level they want.

From my perspective, the frequently asked question of who owns the data is the wrong question. We ought to ask who maintains the data. With our system, who "owns" it is irrelevant, since anybody who wants it and is approved can get it. This system makes data available to anybody anywhere in the world. Each machine is individually addressable and assignable and has its own name, and each user has his or her own sign-on code. The end result is that one computer communications resource is providing information to approximately 10,000 terminals. Basically, the hardware is secondary; primarily what we do is provide a terminal, and the person using that terminal has the smarts of the computer behind it.

One of the problems we used to have involved gateways. In the past there was only one way out of a branch office. That was via a teletype system that was part of our network. Information was passed from functional areas to communications areas and then out. The new system solves that problem. Everyone who has a terminal has a gateway out of the office.

One of the most important management issues is that beyond a certain point you can't pay people more money to do a better job. And people who are capable of doing a better job won't necessarily stay with a company just for more money. To solve the problem you have to provide such people with better resources. Make the same people more productive. Our system does that in a number of areas.

My basic philosophy has always been that the point of origin ought to be the point of entry. If you can accomplish that you can eliminate duplication. This system, obviously, is a natural extension of that philosophy. In terms of word processing, for example, with multiple printers in the branch we can easily separate various functions.

In the area of decision and sales support the system provides the real resource of personal computing at the branch level. Anything that can be done on a personal computer can be done on this system. And much more.

For E.F. Hutton electronic filing of information is part of the electronic mail system and part of the word processing system. It is integrated office automation, and our system does it very logically. Within drawers we have folders, within folders, documents. We can file electronically; we can crumple and uncrumple electronically. We have, in effect, an electronic janitor, and until he empties the electronic wastebasket, we can retrieve. Again, we have all the things personal computers give, plus additional capabilities.

But the administrative support is what sells the system. We can use it as an extension of our operations administration. For example, I can use the system to schedule meetings with people who report to me. I have various options: I can demand a meeting, in which case the computer will cancel any conflicting meetings. Or I can request a meeting, meaning that if these people have open time, the computer will arrange a meeting around their schedules. There will be defaults in which I can get only 18 out of 20 people or 4 out of 5. I also have "public time" in which people can schedule their meetings with me.

The system extends outward as well. We started "Hutton Line" in the state of Florida and expanded it nationally in December 1983. Using a personal computer at home our customers can get direct access to our files. They can use word processing with their account executives, check portfolios, and perform a variety of other functions if they want, including spreadsheet analysis. In short, they have all the functions that are on the personal computer plus the functions on our computer. Thus, the network now extends not only to headquarters, to regional offices, and to

branch offices, but also to our customers. With a million customers, we are looking for a reasonable response of 5,000 clients
by the end of 1984.

This system cost 40 million dollars. For us, the cost-benefits are
really very simple. E.F. Hutton is a firm on the leading edge. As
such, we cannot afford not to have such a system; we cannot afford to be second. Our alternative is not to be in business. Therefore, it is not a question of if, it is a question of who. We chose Data
General because its hardware is significantly more powerful than
the other computers we investigated. We received an operating
system with add-ons and improvements written in to keep us
competitive.

We estimate that we can justify the cost of the system over a
period of three to five years, and we anticipate its life cycle will be
more than seven years. This is unusual because we generally blow
our computers before their leases expire. In fact, I have never
kept a computer until term. The company simply cannot afford to
keep computers that are no longer efficient and economical.

The cost, as far as I'm concerned, is dependent upon the mission. And realizing the mission of an organization raises the issue
of management control. Yet, strangely enough, in all the talk
about personal computers, we don't hear much about managers'
ability to control the work. To me, on-line personal computing
means giving away or abdicating a great amount of responsibility. And, as a businessman, I must wonder how I can control what
I have given away.

For this reason I view the personal computer as a dangerous
weapon and I treat it as such. I think the first and most important
question to ask when considering a personal computing system is,
can I control this? If the answer is yes, and I am satisfied with the
level of control I can exercise over the system, then I would
choose it. If not, I would look for something else. There is a vast
array of options from which to choose. My advice is to take the
best and leave the rest.

Control Through Persuasion

*Allan Z. Loren**

President John F. Kennedy told the story of the leader in the French Revolution who said, "There go my people. I must find out where they are going so I can lead them." This story suggests how CIGNA developed its approach for managing the proliferation of computer technology. It is an approach I call "control through persuasion."

Perhaps the main reason this approach has worked so well is that it grew out of the particular character of our organization. CIGNA is both an old company and a new company. Formed by the largest merger in the financial services industry, CIGNA is a blending of the old Insurance Company of North America (or INA) and the old Connecticut General. It is a diversified financial services organization with over 40,000 people worldwide, $35 billion in assets, 1983 revenues of $12.5 billion, and an after-tax income of $400 million.

CIGNA's Employee Life and Health Benefits Division is the nation's sixth largest provider of group insurance products, which include life, medical, and dental insurance. We are among the largest providers of property and casualty insurance and risk

*Allan Z. Loren is senior vice-president of CIGNA's Systems Division, Philadelphia, Pennsylvania.

management services in the world. We have international operations in 147 countries and the largest investor-owned health maintenance organization in the country.

Ranked as one of the nation's top 10 managers of private pension funds, CIGNA's Employee Retirement and Savings Benefit Division provides a wide range of group annuity products and services and diversified investment vehicles for pension, profit-sharing, and employee-paid investment and savings programs. In addition, CIGNA's Investment Group provides a variety of investment and portfolio management services and is among the nation's top asset management organizations.

As a result of these different operations CIGNA is a melding of distinct and different cultures. Even before the merger, however, the cultures of the predecessor companies were very diverse. Some areas have a centralized vertical management; others have a more bottom-up management style. Different styles are intermingled among the various operations.

Several years ago we became aware of a couple of trends related to technology and to our "customers," that is, our agents and other employees. First, technology was becoming less expensive, more plentiful, and more widely available. Second, a new type of employee/customer was beginning to emerge, younger than average, highly educated, and accustomed to a wide variety of automation capabilities. These new types began populating CIGNA in all of the company's support functions, including marketing, financial analysis, actuarial, and accounting. We concluded that to control and manage the upcoming "technology explosion" and at the same time satisfy the needs of this new employee/customer group, we needed to let customers experiment with technology. Enforcing firm central control and policy would not be possible or desirable given the diverse cultural environment and management styles characteristic of CIGNA. At the same time, of course, we didn't want to abdicate responsibility. The philosophy we came up with for managing technology might be described as "planting the seeds and letting the flowers bloom."

To complement this philosophy we established an End-User Support Group in 1975. This group, comprised of people with a marketing orientation, circulated within the corporation to get close to our new customers and to learn what their needs were. More importantly, this group worked to facilitate the use of technology within the customer community. In effect, they became part of the customer environment.

At the same time large central applications groups within the company were also dealing with this new customer. The support group established close ties with these applications groups and with senior systems management. The close contact among all these groups enabled us to monitor what was occurring and to suggest the most appropriate technology solutions to our customers' problems. To a large extent the support group is really a controlled distribution force, but it doesn't appear so. Its job is to channel our customers' requirements into the mainstream of technology.

The first technical challenge the support group identified was the growth of timesharing. The new customers had already started going outside to get their computational needs satisfied. We facilitated and encouraged this. We also watched what was happening, and guided the customer to certain preferred vendors and applications. Then, when we understood what our customers' real needs were, we created a solution—an internal timesharing system that we call QUEST I. The support group took this internal timesharing system and "sold" it to the customers who had been buying outside timesharing services. There were several advantages to our in-house system. First, our timesharing service was more competitively priced than those outside. Second, we had easier access to corporate databases. Third, we provided better service. In effect, we went into competition with external timesharing organizations and we were very successful.

I must emphasize that we did not mandate the use of this internal timesharing service. However, it was priced and packaged in such a way that customers could not justify going outside and spending more money for the same service. This Milton Friedman-like "free marketplace" philosophy worked quite effectively and as a result most of the outside timesharing was eventually internalized. Some outside databases were being used, however, which we could not internalize. In these cases, processing with outside vendors continued. About four years after we introduced QUEST I we came out with a new product called QUEST II. It has enhanced graphics and language capabilities, offers more software packages, has increased file-handling capabilities, and overall, provides more functions.

When word processing became the "new" technology, we provided our customers with direction by selecting three vendors with whom we would do business. Through consultation and training we channeled these vendor services to our employee/customer.

As a result of the experiences with timesharing networks and word processing systems an interesting situation developed. The support group was able to build a strong relationship with its customer. The group was accepted into the new customer's organization and was considered part of the customer's team. As new technology emerged these customers turned to the support group for advice and consultation.

In addition to forming close ties with the customer community, the support group also maintained its strong links with the applications groups and was able to provide these groups with insight into changing customer requirements.

In the late 1970s and early 1980s, when personal computers started to become popular, we made available to customers—on a casual basis—demonstrations of hardware and software and provided people to answer questions. This approach evolved into what we now call our "information centers."

More recently, we established formal Information Centers in a half-dozen locations. These centers were created to provide customers with a central place to get information, demonstrations, guidance, and training on CIGNA's latest technology. Through the centers we were able to channel people in the right direction. In essence, the information centers served as magnets to draw and direct our customers.

This approach was quite successful. We found that many of our customers wanted help, particularly with the proliferation of hardware and software that is being offered. The Information Centers and our end-user support group, with their very close customer working relationships, were able to produce a set of "technology handcuffs." The customer had become dependent on the group and the centers for guidance on technology. From our standpoint this was an ideal relationship because we were able to point the customer in the direction we wanted to go.

As the 1980s rolled around there was a terrific explosion in microcomputers. At CIGNA we experienced some of the effects of this explosion. The Information Centers, which were well structured by this time, served as real magnets for microcomputer users. In fact, the centers became overwhelmed by the number of customers using their services. To deal with this situation, we went from an informal, casual environment to a more structured, institutional one.

We also began to enhance our level of support. We required users of microcomputers to participate in formal training programs on hardware and software. A newsletter was created to disseminate the latest information on microcomputers. An "approved product" catalogue was developed to aid customers in ordering. Because our customers were demanding direction, we began to issue more standards and became more involved in evaluating products and services. We continued to keep the communication lines open in order to improve our ability to control and channel the uses of this technology.

Today the sheer variety of outside software available to our customers is a source of confusion and therefore has become an area of considerable concern for us. To address this concern we plan to establish a software library. We will lend out software that we find acceptable and provide demonstrations of both "approved" and "unapproved" software in order to show the contrast. To set up this library we will need to arrange for national contracts on software, thus reducing costs and avoiding multiple distributions. We believe the library will save money and help reduce the confusion caused by the proliferation of software. We are also considering developing generic software to run on our personal computers and mainframe. We are finding that much of the software being acquired is used for fairly similar functions and we think we could provide internally written software that accomplishes these same functions.

Another support-related enhancement we are considering is the extension of the information center concept to include a computer store. At present, orders are placed with outside vendors who process them and deliver the software and hardware. Our strategy is to internalize this service by having our customers order directly through an Information Center Computer Store. A centralized procurement activity will not only be convenient for our customers but will allow us to control inventory, offer standard services, and keep a handle on our customers' needs.

In addition, the store will improve our visibility in the customer community, provide us with more information on maintenance and performance of equipment, and help us to know our customers' upgrading needs. The store will also give us and our customers more opportunities to exchange information on applications.

To summarize, the technique CIGNA has used to control proliferation includes having a "friendly" and "forgiving" End-User Support Group whose job was to serve as objective advisor and work closely with customers. Support-group members were able to subtly channel customers in the direction we wanted. Today they continue to provide and enhance support through two-way communications, thereby enabling us both to maintain control and to satisfy our customers' requirements.

Index